W9-ADG-495

(Continued from front flap)

What is needed, says Mr. Fry, is "the presence of Christians who, prompted by the Spirit, speak to each other about the graciousness of God and exhibit through mutual confession and exhortation their ultimate loyalty to Jesus Christ as Lord." Moreover, the Christian's faith, though resting upon superlatively historical events, must not be retrospective. He must experience God's redemptive work, as Paul experienced it, as his possession *now* and in the future, and bear witness to that experience, continually renewing and empowering him. Such witness would be teaching of the highest and most truly Christian order. It would, moreover, deliver men and women from their loneliness and rescue them *as persons* from the devastating and factitious forces that in today's society seek on all sides to impel them into anonymous conformity.

Mr. Fry proposes several concrete procedures that would, he believes, help accomplish this result. He is a man of vast intellectual resources and he has had wide experience in Christian education. His writing is vigorous and vernacular, and his book will be read with profit by ministers and teachers of all denominations.

JOHN R. FRY is a native of Arkansas. After serving for five years with the United States Marines, he attended Colgate University and Union Theological Seminary, graduating from both *cum laude*. Being awarded a Kuyler Preaching Fellowship, he pursued one year of graduate studies in the field of New Testament canon. From 1948 to 1956 Mr. Fry served in several Protestant pastorates. He was Associate Editor and then Editor of *Crossroads* and *Westminster Adult Leader,* and later became Associate Editor of *Presbyterian Life.* He is now pastor of the First Presbyterian Church, Chicago, Illinois.

A HARD LOOK

AT ADULT

CHRISTIAN EDUCATION

A HARD LOOK

AT ADULT

CHRISTIAN EDUCATION

By John R. Fry

THE WESTMINSTER PRESS · *Philadelphia*

COPYRIGHT © MCMLXI W. L. JENKINS

ALL RIGHTS RESERVED — NO PART OF THIS
BOOK MAY BE REPRODUCED IN ANY FORM WITH-
OUT PERMISSION IN WRITING FROM THE PUB-
LISHER, EXCEPT BY A REVIEWER WHO WISHES TO
QUOTE BRIEF PASSAGES IN CONNECTION WITH A
REVIEW IN MAGAZINE OR NEWSPAPER.

Library of Congress Catalog Card No. 61–7708

PRINTED IN THE UNITED STATES OF AMERICA

374
F94

245

111534

To my wife Elizabeth

Contents

INTRODUCTION

A score of reliable books on the subject of the Christian education of adults have recently been written. Here is one more in what will undoubtedly prove to be a steady parade of books aimed at serving various efforts to educate adults in the Christian faith. Adult education currently enjoys a growing popularity. It should be popular: those numberless adults in the church who are virtually illiterate and plainly ignorant of Biblical materials no less than of the standard historical substance of the Christian faith present at best a sorry spectacle. Most denominations are almost paranoid about the situation and have swung into far-reaching programs that involve the expenditure of lots of money and that have commandeered some highly skilled leadership. Books designed to guide the education of adults are therefore in need and in vogue. Their authors outline the course that education should take. They advance plans. They analyze the situation. They share hopes.

In at least one sense this book deviates from the normal pattern of usefulness. It has very few hopes to share with the adult educators or educatees who read it. The conduct of Christian education for adults is not viewed here with any special enthusiasm. My point of view, as a matter of fact, contains equal parts of disenchantment and heavily guarded hopes, both of which have grown in the soil of appallingly practical experience. Observation, intuition, and research cooperate in producing a general impression that most of the Christian education of adults conducted by the church today is almost useless. The disenchantment does not arise out of recognizing the disparity between objectives and performance, a remarkable disparity, to be sure. The disenchantment has been provoked by the objectives themselves, the way they are stated, the manner in which they have been arrived at, and the kind of wistful hoping that they are so full of. This book contends that in contemporary argot the present educational program of the church is "square." The book thus features disenchantment.

Disenchantment can be a cheap and painless reaction to a difficult situation. The temptation to despair of the situation and move to pastures that at least have grass in them appears to adult educators as regularly as it does to other human beings. And a few of them have yielded to the temptation. This book may actually encourage a few more to leave the task as hopeless, but it may also encourage the others to have another look before going. In a word, it has some specific proposals to make. These proposals concern the concrete parish situation and have been formulated in such a way that they can be gotten under way in less than a week. They require no fancy program and are modest in scope. Above all, they have been developed in the specific awareness that they are *not* going to revitalize a parish, help adults to grow, or reform the church.

Expecting too much perennially weakens the existing programs of adult education. By its very nature it is, for instance, ill equipped to reform the church. Some adult educators profess to believe in the reformatory powers of their programs. And every educator at least believes in reform as a principle. Who, indeed, can look at the Protestant Church in America without becoming an advocate of reform? The church needs a new reformation, however, far more than it needs new advocates of reform. Calling for a reformation and doing the painfully messy jobs that constitute reforms are mutually exclusive activities. The reformer reforms while the callers for reform call. Adult educators have, to date, been largely among the callers, the viewers-with-alarm, suggesting that great things often occur in churches that seriously attempt to educate their adults. They are expecting too much.

A typical Protestant church has a situation of the following proportions. A regular Sunday morning class of fourteen adults deals largely with the Bible, using, as a guide, denominational curriculum materials. Fifteen adults serve as teachers in the Sunday school. A women's organization serves 40 per cent of the women in the church. A men's organization serves 15 per cent of the men. Junior and senior high youth groups are led by a total of five adults. On occasion the whole congregation worships. Fifteen adults are on the official governing bodies of the church's life. Perhaps an informal study group of eight people meets in various homes each Thursday night. The choir, numbering sixteen adults and two seniors in high school, also meets on Thursday night. And a couples group, whose membership fluctuates between twenty and thirty, meets each month.

This church offers a variety of adult education programs. Some are formal and some informal. Many people, perhaps as many as 65 per cent of the congregation, have some affiliation with a group in which adults learn something or talk over something or do something that concerns the Christian faith. Obviously the Sunday school does not do all the educating, or even half of it. The other organizations involve most of the adults and in the most significant ways. Any one adult in this church has abundant opportunities to confront the Christian faith in important ways. The possibilities exist.

With the exception of the formal Sunday school class and the informal study group, none of the organizations in which adult education happens think of themselves as having educational responsibilities. They are organized for other purposes, such as to sing, to teach children, to handle the affairs of the church, to meet socially, or to advise young people. Any educating they do is gratuitous and frankly accidental. Now, adult educators ask, what would happen were we to show all these organizations that they do have educational responsibilities which mesh with the explicit programs of adult education? Wouldn't this church become fundamentally more aware of itself as a church with a ministry and a mission? Candor prompts the response that the educators do not envision, inasmuch as the questions they ask are rhetorical. This church conceivably might become more aware of adult education and probably would organize a committee to correlate the various adult educational activities. No evidence exists to suggest that adult education makes any appreciable impact on the direction and thought of a church about itself, its ministry, and its mission. Theoretically, adult education *should* actually transform the life of this typical church, but the way it presently is being conducted shows that it isn't transforming the church and more knowledge about adult education offers no likelihood that the situation soon will change.

Perhaps the chief problem in the church is, as adult educators often claim, adult education. That question can be debated. Were it granted the status of being the number-one problem, programs created to grapple with the problem would tend to become part of the problem instead of a clear answer to it. The typical church, for instance, does not see presently that adult education is a problem. The adults do not admit that they need educating. The organizations of the church are not conscious of having done a poor educational job and for that reason would not accept kindly any suggestion that organizational life be refocused. The official governing bodies of the church would be hard to convince. The pastor himself would likely take a strong adult education emphasis as a personal threat because it would imply that he had not been doing his job.

In order to deal with gross ignorance in this typical church, new educational groups could be devised and all existing organizations charged with new responsibilities only if the church could be made to see that it had a problem. But is this not the underlying problem? The church does not see that it is ignorant and needs educating. Adult education would have to be sold to this church by enthusiasts and experts. The people would have to be talked into it, persuaded that they will receive personal benefits from the experience. The church people, after all, fit appeals from the church into a vast network of appeals from other sectors of their social and economic life. The motion picture theater gets them to a movie with this flaming lie: "The audience was jolted as if they'd been sitting for two hours in an electric chair." (An advertisement for *Look Back in Anger*.)

Competition in the open market for the time and interest of the adult demands tactics of the same nature, if not extent—namely, the church is forced to lie somewhat. It must convince the adult, not that he is ignorant and needs education, but that he is going to have a good time or be jolted or energized or stimulated or—at the very least—socialized.

To tell the individual adult that study is going to be "fun" commits the educational program to a course that cannot thereafter be independent. It must in effect be fun in order to be a success. What does this do to the ignorance? Very little, if anything. It may actually become complicated with fun and a little bit of knowledge, so that it becomes even more obscure—hence, problematic. A program of adult education therefore does not necessarily solve the problem of ignorance but may add to it. The church gains, not education, but one more programmatic concern, and the 20 per cent of the adults in the church who generally hold *any* activity together have to be rallied to the support of one more thing.

The church will not be reformed or transformed by adult education no matter what its exponents claim or expect. The church is not open to its "future of grace"—a term that will presently be developed at some length. It is oriented to its past; its present is filled with the contents furnished by tradition. That is the problem. In one sense of the word, being closed to a future of grace is ignorance, but in order to use the term the qualifying adjective "willful" must also be used.

The church is destructively, perversely, tragically, malignantly, willfully ignorant. Such ignorance, because it is willful, cannot be touched by knowledge or slyly converted by creative group experiences. It is rebellious and defensive. Adult educators not aware (ignorant?) of its reigning power in the church either construct meaningless programs or give up on adult education in disenchantment.

The purpose of this book is rather simple: to deal straightforwardly with the adult education that is possible beyond disenchantment. Two areas of Biblical thought need analysis, along with some features of existing program, before specific proposals in due time can be properly considered.

Were I to make public acknowledgment of indebtedness to those who have most helped me write the book I would have to mention a great many dignitaries in the church and functionaries in adult education who have quite unintentionally led me to views directly opposite their own. I am nonetheless thankful for their views and for the opportunity afforded me by The Westminster Press to point out that—the emperor doesn't have any clothes on.

I have not the least doubt that every one will, with respect to ten of his acquaintances, let us say, be able to hold fast to the view that they are not Christians in the New Testament sense, and that their lives are not even an effort in the direction of becoming such. But when there are 100,000, one becomes confused. . . . They tell a ludicrous story about an innkeeper, a story, moreover, which is related incidentally by one of my pseudonyms, but I would use it again because it has always seemed to me to have a profound meaning. It is said that he sold his beer by the bottle for a cent less than he paid for it; and when a certain man said to him, "How does that balance the account? That means to spend money," he replied, "No, my friend, it's the big number that does it."[1]
—*Sören Kierkegaard.*

[1] Sören Kierkegaard, *Attack on Christendom* (The Beacon Press, Inc., 1956), p. 30.

Chapter 1

A GROUP IS A GROUP

IS A GROUP

One of the remarkable features of the new look in adult education is the attention given to the learner and to the process of learning. A commonplace in the general literature is the recollection that until recently hundreds of books had been written on teaching for every one book on learning. Acquisition of psychological skills has played some part in the educator's recent interest in the learner. Now the educator can find out something about learning. But the interest in learning and the learner is not merely a correlative development of sophistication in the use of psychological measuring and sounding devices. It somehow fits in with the general ruddy persistence of the educator in building a more responsible, healthy, and informed society. He has high hopes for the learner and his learning, which means that the learner has now become the chief figure in education—next, of course, to the expert.

A reliable introductory book to the whole field of what is loosely and can at best be called "group dynamics" concludes with an adumbration of the usual questions that are posed to the experts in the field. One of the questions reads as follows:

Isn't there a danger that all this emphasis on group behavior will lead to a loss of individuality—that "group think" will take over?

The expert, in this case Malcolm Knowles, answers this oft-asked question in a way to which we should pay careful attention:

> To the social scientists this is almost the "unkindest cut of them all." For they know, from their study of groups, that (1) as life becomes increasingly complex individuals become increasingly interdependent and must inevitably do more and more of their work in groups, and (2) nothing can be more tyrannical than a group whose members are unsophisticated about its dynamics. Indeed, probably the best way to preserve individuality is to give every individual the knowledge and skills necessary to diagnose and withstand the forces toward conformity and at the same time to express his individuality constructively. The leaders of group dynamics research and theory have made a special point of trying to disseminate their knowledge widely, and the leaders of applied group dynamics have made a point of training *all* group members, not just selected leaders.[2]

Mr. Knowles's answer is representative of the kind of answer that might be expected from any expert in the field. Some point-by-point exegesis of the answer may then prove profitable. First, we should notice that the question is not answered. The question asks specifically about a danger. The answer specifically justifies the experts without mentioning the danger, except, by inference, to pass off its possibility as an unkind cut. The justification proceeds as follows: (1) The experts—in the study of *group* dynamics—*know* that more and more work is going to be done in groups and that, *therefore,* people ought to know what happens in groups. As a matter of fact, the experts do not *know* this at all. It is at best a mere guess. (2) The experts have done the best they can to let a lot of people know what they know and have concentrated training on *all* group

[2] Malcolm Knowles, *Introduction to Group Dynamics* (Association Press, 1959), pp. 74, 75.

members that they have had anything to do with. The tone of the answer awakens all sorts of doubts that were not originally present. Is the best that the experts can do enough? Have not the bulk of the group members whom the applied experts have dealt with been, as a matter of fact, leaders of other groups which on a more local level are finally composed merely of learners? Isn't the learner who is in a tyrannical, unknowing group as well off as a learner in a knowing group? What good is the knowledge about how groups function unless the knower is a group leader, or an expert?

Group dynamics has probably contributed more to individuality than to the loss of it in American life, but when left to its own resources it seems uneasy about being questioned on the subject and, as we have seen in Mr. Knowles's representative answer, is downright defensive on this score. Here, perhaps, lies a clue for our understanding of the direction, course, and possible dead ends that exist in group dynamics, especially as it manifests itself in adult education in the churches. There seems to be a "sneaking suspicion" among the Christian education experts that some of the criticism that is voiced against group dynamics has a point, but the suspicion cannot be given a name, so it is put away with a somewhat defensive justification of the good things that group dynamics can accomplish. Furthermore, I have yet to find an unqualified group dynamics enthusiast. The more favorable toward the subject always make some grave reservations. The lukewarm intimate that they do not believe in it much and find it either boring or demonic, despite the palpable fact that when in group situations they betray a lot of knowledge of and considerable skill in groupsmanship. Even the rabid anti-group dynamics man is not above resourcefully using groups to his own advantage. The clue, to be clear at last, is that, for the real thinking man in the church, the field of group dynamics is not quite respectable, as it surely is not among humanities professors in American—and English —universities. An Englishman, Malcolm Bradbury, in his novel about English university life, *Eating People Is Wrong*, has qualified as the unkindest cutter to date in a dialogue about group dynamics that proceeds along these lines. Jenkins, a sociologist, is talking to Treece, a professor of English literature.

"Let me tell you about group dynamics—that's what I'm trying to get them to start up here, you know."

"What is it?" asked Treece.

"It's a study of social abrasions that are in-built into every group situation. You know how you feel uncomfortable at parties if you've forgotten to fasten your fly? Well, that's group dynamics. It's a new field. At Chicago we were doing experiments to show that the physical constitutions of rooms had a big effect on the people who used them. We were doing some experiments with conferences for the Pentagon. You know how at conferences it's usual to use two tables set in a T shape? Well, we were able to prove that certain seats at the table were actually dead seats and that because of various factors—not being able to see the chairman's face in order to observe his reactions, and so on — the people sitting in them were virtually excluded from useful participation in the conference. A similar problem arose with the entry of people into the room. We found that some had to come in first and others last. . . . Well, we knew that, of course, but we found that this tended to dramatize latent status problems. That is, people uncertain about their status in relation to others present were made aware of the quandary when it came to the problem of whether to enter the room first, or in the middle, or last. So, you see, we were able to make some useful recommendations. But the feeling that's left is that if only social engineering can get around to enough things, life will be a bowl of cherries."

Treece said: "I hope you don't mind me asking this, but what were the recommendations that you made?"

"The recommendations?" asked Jenkins. "Well, actually what we recommended was that conferences should use a circular table, and a circular room, and a separate door in the wall for each participant. I don't know whether the Pentagon are actually using this yet, but I fancy they will."

"I see," said Treece. "I see." He turned and looked around the room, with a mystified and oddly tired eye; if all the chairs had been filled with horses instead of lecturers and professors taking coffee in their matitudinal quiet, it would have seemed no odder to him than the conversation from which he had just emerged, as from a long black tunnel. Are there, then, he asked with a mind that seemed over the last few minutes to have grown quaintly old-fashioned, in the cast of some barbarian confronted with Athens at its heyday—are there, then, people who do *that* and call it thought?[3]

The high glee with which this little passage has been quoted among a certain species of American intellectual furnishes an index of sorts to the disdain in which the subject is held in other than sociological quarters. Educational specialists in the church, like many other Americans, have been especially sensitive about espousing "non-O.K." causes. The point can be put this way: While in the conduct of their duties as educational consultants and publishers of educational literature these specialists employ many techniques that they have learned from group dynamics, most specialists hold serious intellectual doubts about group dynamics as a movement and may, on occasion, voice strong opposition to group dynamics as such. They have what could be called a mixed mind. The actual education that is being conducted in the local churches presents an assortment of amateurish, old-fashioned, professional, and uneasy use of some techniques that come out of group dynamics research. The assortment defies comprehension and clear analysis, yet the myriad kinds of group situations should serve to set the minds of the most ardent anti-group dynamics people at rest. Group dynamics has *not* gotten into the churches, in spite of the stout and confused efforts by denominational specialists. And the reason for this is not found in intellectual reservations that local churches hold, but simply in plain old-fashioned inertia.

Resorting to all kinds of reported experiences, and experiences in which I have been leader, member, trained, trainer, and observer, and relying principally upon concrete study situations in local churches, four basic, identifiable patterns of groupiness can be defined. (There may be groups which do not, of course, fit any of these patterns.)

3 Malcolm Bradbury, *Eating People Is Wrong* (Alfred A. Knopf, Inc., 1960), pp. 19–20.

The Standard Situation

The standard, old faithful backbone of the churches' adult educational program is the Sunday morning adult class. In the majority of cases this class is known as a Bible class. It functions, like the liturgy, as a part of the church's tradition and stands about as little chance of being critically evaluated. Although local traditional mores vary widely, the conduct of a typical session goes along predictable lines. The class first enters into a devotional period that is at times quite elaborate, and in a few instances as simple as an opening prayer. The elaborate services often feature two hymns (in a large number of churches these "hymns" are inspirational-type gospel songs), responsive reading, a long prayer, the Lord's Prayer, and a Scripture reading related to the announced educational purpose of the class. A few announcements may be made about general church matters or class affairs. At this point the teacher takes over. Note: The devotional leader and the teacher may be the same person, but if so, he and the class recognize that he is functioning in two capacities. Note also: The devotional period often is conducted in the presence of the entire Sunday school.

The teacher's main job is to make a speech on a subject that has been determined by the curriculum material the class is using, the part of the Bible being studied, or a subject in not a few cases of the teacher's own weekly choosing. This speech is the main event. Experienced "teachers" with some suasive powers have been known to compete so favorably with the minister of the church that the class members come to class instead of to the congregational worship, claiming that they "get more out of it."

Generally the teacher asks for questions at the end of his speech. Often no questions are raised. The normal situation would see three or four information-type questions asked, each occasioning a minor speech in return. A closing prayer—sometimes a hymn and prayer—conclude the class session.

The class session, the teacher's speech, the material being used for study—Bible or Bible-centered curriculum—is known in this standard situation as the "lesson." That is the important word, and will not be replaced easily. The word "lesson" calls to mind the old-time schoolroom in which the students recited the lessons that they had learned on the previous night. A lesson refers to a specified body of content that is learned, i.e., memorized or somehow gotten inside, so that it can be gotten back out before the teacher-examiner. In the beginning of adult education in the Protestant churches, this general format was adopted with certain decisive refinements. The lesson was not to be learned altogether by the class member during the week before a class session. It was actually learned when the teacher explained it. *Then* the class member was prepared to recite, the teacher-examiner asking questions to verify the fact that the class member had learned the lesson.

Standing beside modern educational practice, the lecture-recitation method looks both primitive and ineffective. The lesson, whether it be a series of arithmetic problems or a parable of Jesus', can be memorized with some effort, but not really learned. Even when it is explained forcefully by a teacher, the best the student can do is play back the teacher's explanation—if he has paid close attention. A lesson, when thought of as a series of words to be made available to a teacher upon examination, is a foreign body that only festers if not expelled soon. Furthermore, the widespread use of the word "lesson" indicates a serious theological deficiency in the standard situation. Words from the Bible and about the Bible are spoken by an authoritative figure (who often has an extraordinary acquaintance with Biblical materials) in such a way that they will prove helpful to the class member in the conduct of his everyday life. The lesson is for life. However, unless the teacher possesses great wisdom, resourcefulness, and ingenuity, the everyday-life problems that these class members have right now are not dealt with simply because the format does not allow the class member to speak up. He is supposed to cogitate on the lesson in the light of his life. The whole process is carefully stylized and follows unspoken rules that forbid the raising of momentous, hence, genuine, personal problems. The teacher may inveigh against materialism or alcoholism or raise personal theological grudges but does not mention the "aches" in the members' lives.

Judged by minimal norms of good learning and effective teaching, the standard situation can only be called horrible. A denominational specialist who has just returned from "the field," where he has observed a number of these standard situations, looks to the techniques of group dynamics with surprising openness. His intellectual reservations wilt pretty quickly in the glare of this kind of situation. He is, in a word, prepared to go all the way or do anything in his desperation to break up the old and ring in the new. And who can blame him?

The Souped-up Standard Situation

As can be imagined, the reservoirs of resistance to the new are virtually limitless. The standard situation has become a fixture of Protestant life, particularly in rural and other, older well-established churches. It does not submit to evaluation, criticism, or contrived changes in format. But it has, in spite of itself, undergone some slight alterations here and there, largely because of the Herculean efforts of pastors or enthusiastic laymen.

In the souped-up standard situation, the class meets on Sunday morning, retains its name, but has dropped or severely pruned the devotional period. The teacher takes over quickly and gets down to business, which consists of explaining a body of material, commenting on it, and leading into it in such a way that the class will become interested enough to talk. The influence of the group dynamics people can be seen immediately. The teacher attempts to enlist the conversational efforts of every class member (except the congenitally silent). The teacher's souped-up goal is good discussion, understanding by this: a full voicing of class opinions, reservations, experiences, and so on. Teachers seldom come to adopt these goals by themselves. Usually they have submitted to the suggestions of the curriculum materials, which help and urge the teacher to adopt strategies designed in order to provoke discussion. Likewise, there is seldom much subtlety in the way good discussion is imagined or planned for. The teacher in this situation feels that the session is successful if the people have talked and, conversely, that a session is poor if the people have not talked.

A Midwestern teacher reports a successful session on the study of the medieval doctrine of the sacraments. Using a curriculum article to stimulate the interest of the class, she led the class members to think of the form and meaning of the administration of the Lord's Supper in their own local church. This thinking together led quickly to a comparison of the Protestant and Roman Catholic churches. The class was enthusiastic in slaying the Catholics and heroic in defending the Protestants. After the opening statement by the teacher, the class members heard no more about the doctrines of Ratramnus, Radbertus, or Innocent III. These had acted as a springboard into areas where there was interest and capacity for conversation. Although each class member had a copy of the article on the medieval sacramental system, and was supposed to have read it before the session, the article was bypassed in favor of talkable points. The teacher, recall, reported on this session favorably.

Clearly, the souped-up standard situation shows improvement. The long speech has vanished. The class member feels more relaxed about speaking out. A wider variety of subjects (*ipso facto*, more interesting subjects) come into discussion. Above all, the heavy-handed moralism of the standard situation is vitiated. The lesson does not have to be learned, although even in the souped-up situation the sessions must be considered meaningful for everyday life by the class members in order for the class to prosper. It is still a class, but not built in the image of the rural school. The souped-up situation resembles the high school social science class a day or so before school is out. The exams are finished; the texts have been put away;

the projects are complete; so students and teacher talk pleasantly with each other.

Of course, the teachers account for the style in each situation. Teachers who are a little uneasy about all the talk may exercise their prerogatives by doing some old-fashioned straight teaching. Teachers who are intuitively good at sensing the drift of a discussion often lead their classes to appreciably new insights into an issue. Most teachers, however, seem relieved that they no longer have to prepare a long speech and so adopt discussion goals readily as a concession to their intellectual laziness. On the whole, a group dynamics expert observing a typical souped-up standard situation would be appalled by what passes for discussion, by the inept amateurish leader, and by the inefficiency of the group in breaking through its stereotype about itself. Mr. Knowles would call this a "tyrannical group."

The Breakaway Group

At no place in the local church has group dynamics scored heavily. But the small groups meeting at nontraditional times and in an informal atmosphere indicate that some impact has been made. These groups more often than not have been formed at the urging of a pastor or educational materials that place a premium on the values of individual member participation in discussion. The large-group Sunday morning session cannot, in the eyes of the experts, offer the individual opportunities for genuine self-expression, or offer the group opportunities to design for itself adequate goals. The forty- or fifty-minute hour is too short. The situation is too formal. The people, being bound psychologically to a particular understanding of learning, cannot allow themselves to speak freely or to respond freely to one another. Therefore, the experts urge, the study situation should be moved to a week night (or morning, in some cases), into private homes if necessary, in order to stimulate informality and to afford longer session periods in case the discussion extends itself.

The breakaway group has ever in its collective consciousness the notion that it is different. The group maintains a certain pride in being nontraditional and discussion-centered. Group members are quite apt to boast that "anything goes in our group." They express the feeling that they are doing a good thing by having broken away. They often pay tribute to the skill of the group leader who forces them to think for themselves, and who will not give his own mind on a subject because he might thus prejudice the discussion. Moreover, the group members come to enjoy the camaraderie of the being together, attending the meeting even if they have not read the agreed-upon material, because, as they put it, "We don't want to miss anything."

The leader most often found in these breakaway groups has picked up the idea of strictly permissive leadership. He does not "give his mind." He goes with the discussion, questioning discussants in order to help them clarify their own thinking, often engaging in subterfuge for the purpose of exposing buried issues. His job seems to be simply that of a manager. He permits and arranges and enables but is not himself a group member who learns. Measurement of his effectiveness, in his terms, demands looking at the cohesion of the group, the enjoyment that the group experiences in discussion, and group appreciation of his leadership.

The material for study may or may not be Bible material, but it is subtly framed in a notion that whatever is being studied will somehow contribute to knowledge of the Bible. The Protestant unconscious drives unerringly toward Bible study, no matter what a particular book or series of curriculum articles may be about. The breakaway group sticks closely, therefore, to religious matters. It often uses denominational curriculum materials. Most often it engages in specific Bible study, using commentaries, study guides, or a text in conjunction with selected portions of the Bible. A favorite kind of study material for the breakaway group is represented by short, easily read books on theology such as J. B. Phillips' *Your God Is Too Small,* the ten titles in the Layman's Theological Library, the Abingdon Press *I Believe* series, the World Perspective Series, and so on. The material stays within the orbit of conventional religious concern: personal piety, churchmanship, Bible knowledge, doctrine, and church history. And the general permissiveness with which the group is managed tends to short-circuit the material, anyway, because what is most important about this sort of group is not what it studies but how it talks. The souped-up standard group finds the fact of group talking important. The breakaway group finds the *style* of talking important.

Example: A Wednesday evening Bible study group meets in one of the parlors of a large suburban church. The group had been meeting weekly for nearly three months. The composition of the group tells us something about what happened one particular evening. Three members of the group thought of themselves as liberated Protestants. They could view without alarm the idea that the Old Testament had been written, edited, and re-edited by men. For instance, they had not flinched at the notion that Adam and Eve were not historical individuals. Two group members were in the process of being liberated. The facts, the leader's position, and the strength of the three previously mentioned group members' position were working inside these two against their inherited ideas about the authorship and nature of the Old Testament materials. Two other group members were fighting the results of Biblical scholarship with every emotional resource that they could command. Yet two other members were intent on finding personal, "spiritual" meaning in any Biblical text, following a method of Bible study learned at a Quaker training school. The leader had not overtly disclosed his position, although he was in sympathy with the position of the curriculum materials that were being used as a basis for the study.

The curriculum article for the particular meeting with which we are concerned described the contest between Elijah and the priests of the Baalim on Mt. Carmel. The leader began the meeting by asking the group members to recapitulate the contents of the curriculum article. One of the liberated members elaborated the article's contention that the I Kings story repre-

sents a mythical dramatization of Elijah's revolutionary proph-
etism. The two anti-scholarship people thundered out against
the position of the article and the group member who expressed
it. The two other liberated members joined the fray. Soon
Elijah had been put aside in order to argue in full heat the
authorship and intent of I Kings. The two spiritualists came
into the discussion with, to the discussion, irrelevant comments
about the *contest meaning* of the Elijah story, pointing out its
intensely personal nature, even though in terms of the formal
purpose of the evening these interjections were the only relevant things being said. No one won the argument. The leader
seemed content with this fact and did not feel any compulsion
to repoint the argument toward the specific I Kings material
itself. Failing this, the group members began hammering out
a new issue: Billy Graham. Of course, there *is* a deep theological connection between positions on the work of Billy Graham
and positions on the Carmel episode. Perhaps the leader perceived the connection and was happy to let the discussion move
into this modern area, but ostensibly he would have been as
contented had the group been discussing the work of Li'l
Abner.

The formal session closed with the leader noting the nature
and extent of material to be covered in the following session.
At this point the group members began abruptly to talk to each
other about how much fun they had had, how interesting the
session had turned out to be, with not one word of sorrow for
the jilted Elijah left ninety minutes before on Mt. Carmel.

The similarities between this session and the session which
on a Sunday morning evaded the medieval sacraments are obvious. Neither group actually discussed the material. One
group was happy to find itself talking and the other group
was content to argue sharply over an assorted number of
subjects. But there is a remarkable dissimilarity. The breakaway group is much more pretentious, has learned to think of
itself as *avant-garde,* daring, and even a little risqué. The members of this group, despite fierce disagreements, display the
characteristics of an in-group; they are unanimous in their faint

disdain of the theologically unknowing, namely, everybody else in the church.

One further point: at the end of this group's life the two members who held conservative views had succumbed intellectually to the emotional pressure put upon them to conform, though emotionally they had by no means deserted the position with which they had begun. The breakaway group frequently produces pressures toward achieving something like a consensus, although, as in the group we have noted, the consensus is phony and for looks alone. The social solidarity seeks the appearance of intellectual sameness and generally, if given enough time, wins.

The Secrets of Jesus Society

There has grown up in the church a mystique about small groups, especially since 1945. The widely popular book by Elton Trueblood, *Alternative to Futility,* has been followed by countless successors, the best of which is John Casteel's *Spiritual Renewal Through Personal Groups* and the latest of which is David Ernsberger's *A Philosophy of Adult Christian Education.*[4] Trueblood's alternative turned out to be the cell group. This was his formal proposal to the church in the face of shattering postwar depersonalization. Through the cell group the church might re-create itself in the image of a New Testament model. The cell group would, in Trueblood's eyes, revive the spiritual intimacy of the New Testament groups. Although proposals have grown more specific and some of the goals have been scaled down a bit over the years, the latest cell group enthusiasts continue to hold out for the same Trueblood alternative to the same postwar futility.

Special words in the small group mystique are "discipline," "redemption," "reconciliation," "*koinōnia,*" "transformation," "re-creation," and "renewal." These words are used to describe

---

[4] Elton Trueblood, *Alternative to Futility* (Harper & Brothers, 1948); John L. Casteel, *Spiritual Renewal Through Personal Groups* (Association Press, 1957); David J. Ernsberger, *A Philosophy of Adult Christian Education* (The Westminster Press, 1959).

alternately the goal and the reality of the small group. The objective in view seems to be the creation of Luther's *ecclesiola in ecclesia*. Little churches within the church are better than nothing at all, and, in the framework of a certain reading of the holy history, there never has been anything except the little church within the big church. The little church is the saving remnant, the true apostolic continuum, the true elect, the spiritually enlightened. The big church is for show. It functions like chaff, keeping the good wheat warm. There is, in the literature, some attempt to specify the small group as a cell of true Christianity. Both Ernsberger and Casteel quote a pastor to good effect in making that case. The pastor says:

> The development of small groups in the life of the church is not a gimmick. It is not a technique to add more programs to churches, which, for the most part, are already overburdened with programs. The only purpose is to provide God with an effective channel of communication, whereby he can reveal himself to his people and the gospel can become a living reality. Small groups, if they are to have a place in the life of our church, must be redemptive fellowships of love in which the living Christ can be known. God alone can give birth to such a community. (Ernsberger, p. 106; Casteel, p. 78.)

According to the pastor, and to Ernsberger and Casteel, who cite him with favor, God needs small groups in order to do his work. And yet, small groups *must* be redemptive fellowships which only God can create. This kind of reasoning can lead to but one conclusion. The big all-church group is not getting the job done. Hence: on to small groups. Whether realistic or not, the argument does eventually get around to specifying the small group as the only real church worth talking about. The pastor clinches the case for small groups with this enthusiastic utterance about groups he has known:

> There was no question that some members began to see the Christian faith in a new light, and real changes began to take place in their lives. Perhaps the best explanation is that what had been words about the Christian faith was translated by the group

into concrete reality. Love, acceptance, forgiveness, were no longer "halo words," but living experiences in the relationships of the members of the groups. The words literally became incarnate. People felt that they could be themselves without jeopardy. They could witness to their faith or express their doubts without fear. (Ernsberger, p. 112; Casteel, pp. 69, 70.)

We need not go farther into the case for them, and now we ask: What, empirically, takes place in the small group? The small group demands lay people who have been encouraged in one way or another to want this kind of experience. Either the layman requests such a group from his pastor, or the pastor, aware of the potential in certain laymen, asks them to join such a group. The group needs committed people because the activities of the small group demand mutuality. The group meets in order to pray together, discuss personal problems together, search the Scriptures together, read helpful books together, all within a context that is far beyond first-name informality. Small-group members come to know, via confession, a great deal about others' *psyches*. The group cannot function without such closeness.

Example one: A prayer group meets weekly on Tuesday evenings. It is composed of three couples, a middle-aged maiden, and an elderly widower. They talk about each other. They discuss the problems that each encounters in "the Christian life." The group, formed especially in order to pray, prays for the ill, for the church, and for each other. Devotional manuals are used by the group members, sometimes at certain agreed-upon times between meetings, and the contents of the manual are then discussed at the meeting. The level of intensity is so keen and the commitment so firm that the group does not need any formal leadership. This, however, does not mean that the group is without leadership, because the strongest and/or the wisest does subtly steer the group's life.

Example two: Seven housewives gather on Wednesday mornings for Bible study, led in their study by one of the seven who has had some training and experience in Bible study and small-group work. These women talk about their problems and use the Bible and Bible study as a legitimatizing frame for what otherwise might be thought of as indulging in self-pity and gossip.

Example three: A group of doctors get up early on Tuesday morning and study the relationship of the Christian faith to the practice of medicine. An associate minister of the church leads the study. The doctors have gotten over some initial hesitancy about speaking out with each other before a medical layman, and freely expose him to the interior of their professional and personal lives.

Example four: Five couples study theology and themselves— as couples and as parents—on various week nights, the group meeting in any one of their $30,000 to $40,000 homes. This group reads psychological help articles, self-help books, and formally is attempting through the group to cultivate in the represented homes a Christian atmosphere. The leadership of this group rotates among the couples, as does the meeting place and the preparation of refreshments.

Naming these four groups does not exhaust the variety of small-group life in the churches, but it indicates the specific quality of personal intensity. The people in small groups are attracted to each other as attractive individuals. They come to care for each other, and despite the explicit avowals of the spiritual characteristic of the caring, I have begun to believe that a good deal of physical and intellectual caring goes on too. Fetishlike openness and frankness provokes exactly the kind of spiritual undressing that cannot fail to have libidinous dimensions. Perhaps the incapacity of most small groups to talk publicly about sex as such should be seen as a sign that an honest airing of the subject would reveal too much. The five couples, for instance, talk about some particular problems of "parenting" with ease. They candidly pool their wisdom on how to deal with bed wetting, masturbation, stealing, and so on. Yet the same parents who can openly discuss the fact that one of their sons has been involved with the police because he has been caught stealing in the five-and-ten do not discuss their own personal sex lives. More than traditional modesty is needed to explain the roping-off of this area, and *perhaps* one of the reasons can be found in the danger that the couples perceive in revealing too much about how they "feel" about the non-wives and nonhusbands of the group.

Groups formed along single-gender lines, less obviously erotic because, obviously, homoerotic warmth is less socially acceptable, have more than professional or vocational homogeneity. Men who come together as men, women who meet together as women—divulging secrets, deliberately revealing the underside of their personal lives—*exhibit* what they would find disquieting to have mentioned. While few—if any—directly sexual liaisons result from small-group acquaintance, that potential furnishes the group with much of its "go" power.

Although no significant body of evidence exists to *prove* the presence of deeply libidinous aspects in small groups, which is not surprising inasmuch as sociometry is hardly equipped for this kind of study, the smothering personalness of small-group life leads to the suspicion of its presence. Coupled with the high priority given to "spiritual" (i.e., personal) matters, the intimacy of the small group indicates a high threshold for deliberately sexual discussion and an extremely low threshold for veiled erotic stimulants. Terms like "love," "sacrifice," "union," "slave," when appearing in a religious discussion are capable of carrying a distinctly erotic cargo, especially in a small group that is, member to member, getting and staying close. I am not suggesting that the erotic warmth of the small group is wrong. It is the cement that holds the small group together, no matter what verbal theological claims are made, and that is the point I am trying to make.

The small group is by definition private. It can nourish the values of warm personness only if it is private. The members care for each other. They may later learn to care for others; sometime they may find other neighbors in Christ to love; for now, they have each other. Their discussion of the gospel, therefore, has a kind of private—"for us only"—tone. The world with its monsterlike problems is dyked out. They eventually become societies interested in the secrets of Jesus, resembling the Gnostic groups that flourished in the second century. Neo-Gnostic cells of piety, meeting in $35,000 ranch houses, offer the person direct entry into a religious world of prayer, confession, Bible study, and fellowship, and direct, though temporary exit from the confusion of his own life in the world.

As far as group dynamics is concerned, the small group is close to being a "good" group. Problems of formal leadership are not ordinarily great. Group members relate well and candidly to each other. The goals of these groups are adequately worked out and are being met with passable success. Group members are loyal to the group and find genuine satisfaction in the group activities.

Denominational specialists, too, are happiest with the small group. At every available opportunity they suggest the small informal group as an answer to the educational uselessness of the standard situation. They recommend the small group not only as a means of breaking up a traditional pattern but because the small group has positive values in its own right. Furthermore, the general all-group commitment necessary for the small group solves the often insuperable problem of finding good leaders. And what goes on in the small group is thought to be valuable to the individual member because he is taken seriously. Last of all, the full range of the Christian faith can be studied and lived. Many denominational specialists believe that the small group might be a bridge between the poses and dodges of unsuccessful education today and the new church of tomorrow.

Contrary to appearance, announced purpose, and expectations, the small group is more like Trueblood's cell group than it is the healthy group approved by group dynamics experts. The small group does not, as every group dynamics manual insists, maintain a running critique and evaluation of its own process. Many of these groups have leaders who are ignorant of the basic tenets of group hygiene and leadership. Some groups are not tyrannical; they are vicious. For this reason we should see that group dynamics and the small groups multiplying like hamsters in the church today have little to do with each other. The small group is closer to traditional Protestant piety than it is to Kurt Lewin, and thus closer to the standard situation than to the breakaway group.

The interminable discussions in the ranks of Christian educators over the merits of group dynamics sound academic and hollow when considered against the backdrop of what is actually taking place in the churches. Group dynamics has scarcely touched the churches, and for a very good reason. The whole idea has got to be developed in the churches. Local churches just do not see the need for restructuring their educational program, and heretofore professional educators have been impressive failures in pleading their case before the churches. We have already called attention to this inertia. Now we shall want to look at another phase of the problem. That is the confused mind of the educator. "If the bugle gives an indistinct sound . . . !"

This is the point of confusion: On the one hand the educators want the people in the churches to learn something, and are willing to adopt the techniques of group discussion, use of audio-visual aids, forums, buzz groups, audience feedback systems, problem census devices, brainstorming, workshop methods, or almost anything in order to make learning a possibility—as opposed to the traditional "just sitting." But on the other hand, the methods deemed useful in stimulating learning focus attention on the learner and his needs—as a matter of fact, presuppose a definition of the contemporary adult as a "person." Meeting his needs must be considered a goal as worth-while as affording him an opportunity to learn. We see here the makings of a first-class quandary, *exactly* the quandary that manifests itself in the local church situations. Is good discussion in which every member has made meaningful contributions a legitimate goal for education *in a church?* Should the churches resort to more formal learning situations in which all-class participation is dropped as a goal but in which a studied attempt is made to teach something? Has the church filled its educational obligations in meeting the learner's needs? Are there as yet unexplored connections between the personal fulfillment designed to take place in group life and the traditional evangelical emphases on salvation, redemption, and reconciliation? In other words, can "real sharing" of persons in group relationships be classified as "reconciliation"?

The educators have thus far only discovered the quandary. It goes without saying that they are a long way from finding a way out. The depth of the quandary, however, has not been plumbed. By espousing a change theory of learning, by uncritically accepting the needs definition of the learner, by confusing illiteracy with ignorance, by encouraging neo-Gnostic cell groups—adult educators have tacitly decided that healthy groups are more important than the communication of content. The two possibilities are not exclusive of each other in their minds, but if a fateful choice had to be made, the educators would, in order to be consistent if nothing else, choose the healthy group. We should not be led, therefore, to conclude that the quandary is unreal. Educators are unsatisfied with the idea of a lot of happy church groups in which the members are learning how to live with each other, and little else. The educators desire direct communication of the gospel. But in their arcane commitment to the healthy group they have *perhaps* made the fulfillment of their desires impossible. That is the desolating possibility that every adult educator eventually has to face.

Inevitably and continuously, the forward-driving "I" is sacrificed to the persistent and pressing "they." To the question, "Who is human being?" (*die Frage nach dem Wer des Daseins*) we must answer: the indifferent and anonymous crowd, "*das Man.*" Human being in its everyday mode is promiscuously public; it is life with others (*Mitsein, Mitdasein*), for others (*Fürsorge*). Not only the particular things in my world: the joint to be roasted, the car to be greased, the bills to be paid, but the particular people too concerned with these things: my family who eat the joint, the butcher who provides it, the mechanic who services the car, the salesman who sold it—all these weave round my life, as I around theirs, a net of distraction and betrayal. Though my existence is my own, from my birth to my death, nothing in its humdrum course is truly, properly, authentically, exclusively mine: it is yours, theirs, anybody's.[5]—*Marjorie Grene.*

[5] Marjorie Grene, *Martin Heidegger* (Hillary House, Inc., 1957), pp. 25, 26.

Chapter 2

THE PERSON ENTERS

CHRISTIAN EDUCATION

Adult educators in the church have a mixed mind on group dynamics. But they are unanimous and enthusiastic about the word "person," which denotes the adult of adult education. Among the adults themselves, "person" as a word does not cast any spells of enchantment. "Person" remains for them an ordinary word, approximate in meaning to "self," "individual," "body" (one's "person"), or "hey, you!" But to the educators, those denominational and interdenominational specialists who are employed by the church to produce curriculum and program materials for the churches, the word "person" has secret power and reservoirs of hidden meaning. Through an analysis of the meaning that "person" seems to have we may come a long way in understanding the new look in today's Christian education of adults.

Note: The Christian education of adults is not restricted to the often dismal goings-on in the local church. It has a life of its own among the specialists, as they write to each other about adult education, for each other, and occasionally copy from each other. These specialists are in contact with the local churches, of course, because that is what they get paid for;

therefore we are not going to understand even the local church scene adequately unless we attempt to fathom what loosely— and generously—is referred to as "the philosophy of Christian education of adults." And were we to restrict our investigations to the empirical happenings on the local scene, we would miss the most lively, puzzling, confused part of adult education, that is, those who philosophize and the reasons they cite for using the grand word "philosophy" to describe their theories, ideas, researches, plans, hopes, and random brainstorms. To get to the point: in this and succeeding chapters I shall be dealing more with the intramural talk among experts about education than with local education.

Person as Post-Student

For nineteen hundred years less a decade, adults in the church were thought of as communicants, Christians, saints, and so on. Then in the period 1890 to 1945 a startling development occurred. The adult became a student. He had before that time played the chief educational role in the church as the parent-teacher. He was educated by books, or by art, or by architecture, or by sermons (in the context of the whole liturgy). From these experiences, which were educational only in a secondary sense, the adult learned enough to be able to teach the young. The young grew up, having been previously taught, to appropriate for themselves the Christian message. Then they became teachers. And so on.

At the tag end of the nineteenth century, however, that traditional "parent to child who becomes parent to his child" way of viewing the adult met a challenge in the form of explicit educational classes for adults. The church had maintained a growing Sunday school facility for children and youth for approximately 115 years. To the Sunday school the adult student was then added as a practical concession to the facts. Parents were not teaching their children and youth, because the parents themselves did not know anything. Furthermore, the adults who staffed the Sunday school classes for youth and children needed instruction, while the staffs themselves needed considerable beefing up. And another fact: The great burst of evangelistic, missionary, *and* ecumenical fervor so character- istic of the time led to the creation of down-to-earth *Bible* classes. Protestantism became uneasy, apparently, over the lack of sound Bible knowledge in the laity and did something about it. So, the adult, newly turned student, was more than that. He was a Bible student, a Bible-class member.

Hard upon the advent of the Bible class came writers who prepared materials for the classes to use. The writers had to use some convenient terms in addressing the students, giving instructions, suggesting procedures, and illustrating ideas. So they used the terms "teacher" and "student" or, an interchange- able term, "class member," because of the supposed educational nature of the class. Looking at the early materials used in these classes, one gets the idea that the writers had a pious Protestant in mind when they used the terms "teacher" and "student." Great emphasis was placed on the standard evangelical-moral virtues: thrift, sobriety, doing good, salvation to the heathen, salvation to *anybody,* respect for the church and church work, honesty, faith, believing, witnessing, and being a good disciple. The teacher fell heir to the job of teaching these virtues, and the student was cast in the unenviable role of the taught, the never good enough, the talked at, the absorber of words. Good old automatic Protestant Student was expected to reproduce in daily life everything that he heard on Sunday morning.

It did not work, naturally. That it did not work is a fact of immense historical significance. Because the student did not learn but merely sat and listened; because the teacher had so little room in which to operate—the typical round of possible emphases never exceeding ten basic topics, no matter what Scripture was "used" as a text—that he could not avoid the stigma of being irrelevant and mostly boring; because, above all, the enthusiasm for Bible classes languished—the churches, through the medium of their employed experts, began to revise and update their views on education as such.

Had the churches been content with the Bible class, the

format probably would not have been changed. But local churches and national denominational educators saw that something new had to be tried. At this point, however, the historical ball took a peculiar bounce. While some churches tried to be new by redoubling their traditional efforts and squirting adrenalin into the worn-out classes (bigger and better speakers; brass ensembles; contests; etc.), other churches moved away from the traditional norms toward the new secular adult education that had been rising and flourishing all across American life.

Church educators just had to be impressed sooner or later with the glowing success that secular educators were enjoying. (Read through the *Handbook of Adult Education in the United States*, edited by Malcolm Knowles,[6] and you will be impressed too.) New, unusual, casual, and effective educational opportunities were being offered the American adult in shop, office, university, high school, and home. We are talking now of the late 1920's and 1930's. A variety of organizations were getting into the business of education, organizations such as labor unions; public schools; industry; Federal, state, county, and municipal governments; political parties; and the Y.M.C.A., Y.W.C.A., Y.M.H.A., and Y.W.H.A. And these organizations bore essentially the same thrilling testimony: Adults past their formal education can learn new skills. They are capable of becoming better informed. They can find better ways to manage themselves as they work and play together. Above all they have the capacity to become better—persons! No adult needs to stop learning when he frames his last diploma. He is always learning and should be encouraged to continue his learning in fruitful and creative circumstances.

Well! We do not need much imagination to guess what happened. The denominational educators, and educators who belonged to the old International Society of Religious Education (responsible for the beginning of the *International Journal of Religious Education*), began to find out what was happen-

---

[6] Malcolm Knowles, ed., *Handbook of Adult Education in the United States* (Adult Education Association of the U.S.A., 1960).

ing to adults outside the church. This was a fitting prelude for their consequent attempts to provide adult education in the church with a new look.

Adult education outside the church made a lazy approach to the whole venture. People sat around in groups and talked, or they tried out their skills. They were not taught how to paint, for instance, they were encouraged to paint, literally to apply brush to canvas, with few preliminary words about painting. As a matter of fact, adults were never talked to, they were consulted. When they knew that they needed information, a resource person provided them with information which, because they knew that they wanted it, was promptly learned and put to some perceptible use. The adult engaged in these casual activities did not act like a student at all but rather like a casual, *interested* adult. And the professional educators outside the church made quite a point of knowing the adult learner and of finding out how he learns and how he grows. He is not just a student, a great ear designed for listening to words or all mind designed for tabulating concepts. He is a person, a warm, feeling, thinking, interesting person who is most himself when he can respond normally to other persons with whom he is leagued.

Adult education's initial introduction to the word "person" in that peculiar setting has had profound consequences for the course and style of the Christian education of adults. The educators—not all of them, to be sure—were quick learners. They felt a need, found their new information, and were never quite the same. The adult in their church education was thereafter thought of and talked about as "a warm, feeling, thinking, interesting person who is most himself when he can respond normally to other persons with whom he is leagued."

I have attempted this scandalously abbreviated summary of the historical circumstances that led up to the discovery of the word "person" in order to give flavor and not necessarily to provide the names and numbers of all the players, which facts are available in a number of fully accredited sources. For the purposes of this discussion, this is the important historical fact:

"person" was originally defined in the Christian education of adults as a negative term meaning nontraditional student or post-student. The term came to be used as the best possible word to stand in antithesis to the old-style words, "student" and "class member." "Person" means non-all ear or non-all mind. A person learns. Students are taught. "Person" means that happy creature in the Great Books discussion group and not that bored creature in the Bible class.

The Needs of a Person

The post-student person has needs, a point that the Bible class type of education had not reckoned with. A person does not want answers to questions he is not personally asking. Of what use is information about the geography of Palestine or Paul's second missionary journey if the particular person receiving the information has just lost his job? (Reuel Howe has written a sophisticated statement of this disparity entitled *The Creative Years*,[7] in which he talks through a harassed business executive to the church that has meant so little to *him* as he is and that served his needs so poorly.) The personness of the person, educationally speaking, can be found precisely in his needs. The needs, of course, are real. They often represent painful realities and would not be real unless they had a certain ache potential. Perhaps the educators feel some compassion for the needy person and conceivably weep a few tears while contemplating his lot. This is surmise. Reading the books and pamphlets written by the educators will more likely foster the opposite conclusion. They seem almost gleefully triumphant for having found the needs, because the needs of the person are, conveniently, the chief motivating factors in sound education.

A good dozen books on the subject of the Christian education of adults stress the needs that a person has. Allowing for varieties of expression and order, the needs that appear in these books can be listed in the following way:

[7] Reuel Howe, *The Creative Years* (The Seabury Press, Inc., 1959).

A person needs
—food, sex, and shelter (physical needs)
—growth (more like an urge)
—security (physical and psychological safety)
—new experience (why stay contented?)
—affection (a social need)
—recognition (a psychosocial need).

Naturally, a person does need everything on the list, not always all together or in quite the same way, but nonetheless he needs them. But what is the purpose behind analyzing adult needs? Let the latest manual on adult education that has been published as of this writing answer our question.

> Persons are prior to methods, and the methods we use must be appropriate to their problems and needs. Effective teachers or leaders of adults must know something about the nature of adults as learners—what motivates them, what conditions underlie their effective participation, and what conditions help promote the acceptance of personal responsibility for learning.[8]

McKinley, like the many writers before him who have made a similar sort of introduction, then gets down to the list, although his has a distinctive slant and reflects his own priorities.

The idea behind person-centered learning can be recited with deceptive ease. A "person" "learns" when he is "motivated" "to learn." Therefore, educators will not do very well until they know what motivates the person, and, to follow on, a person is "moved" to learn when he has a need that can be eased by learning. Therefore, theorize the educators, analysis of needs should improve understanding of motivation, which should produce better learning. And in theorizing about the needs of the person, some of the shine begins to wear off the recognition of the learner as a person. The more his needs are analyzed the more he seems to be a learner, after all, someone to be taught, motivated, energized, helped to participate, analyzed, and just plain changed (see Chapter Three for a longer dis-

---

[8] John McKinley, *Creative Methods for Adult Classes* (The Bethany Press, 1960), pp. 11–12.

cussion of this particular point). Such are the vicissitudes encountered by the person in adult education. He is first elevated from humdrum boredom to a pinnacle of promise only to be dissected in full public view.

Psychology and sociology provide the educator with his dissecting tools. Literally thousands of research projects have been cited by educators in their efforts to appropriate the findings of these eager investigators into the individual and social psyche of the person. A random example may show what I mean. One educator cites a study by W. I. Thomas, *The Unadjusted Girl*, in order to get his bearings in the analysis of the adult need for security. Christian educators, while sympathetic to this sort of thing, are ultimately condescending because they believe themselves to have a more reliable way for getting at adult needs, namely, the Christian tradition itself. So when we consider the *Christian education* of adults, we should not be surprised at the innovations that appear in descriptions of the person and his needs. Although the Christian lists of needs, when translated, are identical to the lists produced by secular educators, on the surface they are sicklied o'er by the pale cast of religion.

What does the person need, according to Christian education lists?

—love	—responsibility
—community	—self-understanding
—acceptance	—neighbor understanding
—security	—community understanding
—affection	—world understanding

Not every one of these needs is a felt need. Very few persons feel a need for world understanding. But within the purview of the educator, that is nevertheless a *real* need. A person who does not understand the world, in other words, is not quite all the person that he might be. Whether felt or latent, the needs of the person are used to the same ends as the needs designed by secular educators. Out of the awakened need proceeds the motivation for learning. Knowing the needs helps the educator to trigger needs, so that education happens. And the Christian educator works in the same effective way that his secular tutor works.

A world affairs group leader in a university extension program and an informal theological discussion group, meeting in the local church, work the same way (in the eyes of the Christian educator), although the content used for the discussion differs. Attractive publicity plus person-al contact awakens the feeling in the person that he wants to know about this matter. He goes to the group, and needs that he was not particularly feeling are met, so he stays and learns, not only about world affairs or theology, but about himself, other group members, the dynamics of human relations—in the end becoming a better, well-informed, needs-met person.

This is all very laudable. But could a plain adult without analyzed needs go through exactly the same experience? Probably not. The theoretical understanding of the adult person, his needs, motivation, and learning, has produced both the secular and the ecclesiastical group. No person, no needs. No needs, no motivation. No motivation, no education. This crisp rundown helps us to see in some measure why the word "person" enjoys such prestige among the experts.

Person as Thou

In discussing the reasons for the fondness that Christian educators express for the word "person," we have been concentrating on the affiliation of Christian education with secular education in general, which, after all, did teach the Christians to respect the person, even though the respect has turned out to have certain utilitarian features. This is only half the story. All the while that Christian educators have been dallying with the secular educators they have been concerned simultaneously with new developments along the personality frontier and in the field of rejuvenated Protestant Biblical theology—both of which have had some helpful—useful—things to say about the person.

The Christian educators have learned on the personality

frontier, i.e., in the field of relationship psychology broadly known as interpersonalism, that the person is a mystery. He is furthermore a religious mystery as C. J. Jung points out in his *Modern Man in Search of a Soul*, or a psychosexual mystery, as Sigmund Freud points out in his *Introductory Lectures in Psychoanalysis*, and more so in his *New Introductory Lectures on Psychoanalysis*. He does not understand himself, as Franz Kafka points out in *The Trial*, as Picasso points out in his *Guernica*, and as playwrights Tennessee Williams and Eugene O'Neill point out in their numerous plays. And the mysterious person is up against enormous social pressures, as David Reisman points out in *The Lonely Crowd*, William Whyte, Jr., points out in *The Organization Man*, and Vance Packard points out in his trilogy, *The Hidden Persuaders*, *The Status Seekers*, and *The Waste Makers*. We live in an "I-It" world, as Martin Buber points out, while actually we should live in "I-Thou" relationships.

The ironic intent of the previous outlandish, name-dropping, bibliographical paragraph should not obscure the solid point it attempts to establish. In Christian education books, manuals, pamphlets, and articles, the subject of person is dealt with in just that way. Various educators go at their business in differing ways, but among themselves they have developed a standard repertoire of books and authors (with the exception of *Guernica*, by Picasso, out of Tillich) that are generally mentioned. The typical work proceeds to establish these facts:

1. The person is a mystery.

2. The person is being assaulted in today's society. (Upstage lights. Enter Buber.)

3. The person must be respected.

Eventually the work at hand shows its true colors and we are led to see that the mysterious person to be respected forms the backbone of good relational communication, which in turn is the backbone of every sound procedure in Christian education.

Martin Buber's lyrical "philosophical-religious poem," as its translator calls *I and Thou*, bears some hard witness upon the sort of educational programs that the educators have in mind for the mysterious person. At one point Buber says:

But this is the melancholy of our fate, that every *Thou* in our world must become an *It*. It does not matter how exclusively present the *Thou* was in the direct relation. As soon as the relation has been worked out or has been permeated with a means, the *Thou* becomes an object among objects—perhaps the chief, but still one of them, fixed in its size and its limits. In the work of art realization in one sense means loss of reality in another. Genuine contemplation is over in a short time; now the life in nature, that first unlocked itself to me in the mystery of mutual action, can again be described, taken to pieces, and classified— the meeting point of manifold systems of laws. And love itself cannot persist in direct relation. It endures, but in interchange of actual and potential being. The human being who was even now single and unconditioned, not something lying to hand, only present, not able to be experienced, only able to be fulfilled, has now become again a *He* or a *She*, a sum of qualities, a given quantity with a certain shape. Now I may take out from him again the color of his hair or of his speech or of his goodness. But so long as I can do this he is no more my *Thou* and cannot yet be my *Thou* again.[9]

The person as Thou, to be blunt, looks well in print but bears no resemblance to Buber's expression *Thou*. Buber knows of a "melancholy fate" that is not often listed by Christian educators as a component of the mysterious person. They betray their distrust of Buber's whole point of view by assuming that if a person is treated like a Thou, respected for his Thouness, a fundamental relationship will be established, the walls of separation and itness will fall away, golden trumpets will sound, and—the relationship will continue. Buber is not needed here. Empirical facts are enough to cite against such a notion.

But the person has not been described as a Thou by Christian educators merely in order to sound good. Thou is used instinctively to designate a difference that the educators see in the life that should characterize the Christian community in its group relations. In modern America the person *is* treated like a thing. He *is* badgered by monstrous forces that seem intent on destroying his individual worth. The quality of his

[9] Martin Buber, *I and Thou,* 2d ed. (Charles Scribner's Sons, 1958), pp. 16–17.

everyday life turns out to be depersonalized, quantitative, ex-asperatingly like the life of his next door neighbor—with all signs pointing to worsening trends. Against such a backdrop the educators use Thou as the most splendid word they know in order to specify the sort of personal relations that should exist in the church and its educational programs. Here in the church, at least, a haven should be maintained for deeply satis-fying personal meetings and for the fulfillment of searching personal relationships. In the world the person is given a worth in terms of dollars or the status symbols that his dollars can purchase. In the church the person should be honored for what he is and treated as a Thou.

Now we come to see another important reason for the warmth that educators radiate in the presence of the word "person." By the use of that word they can rightly establish the church as a bulwark against depersonalized living and can communicate to groups a new, *sacred* understanding of them-selves as protectors of the Thou. The melancholy fate of the educators seems to be that the church does not heed the com-munication. Church groups perhaps should be a haven and occasionally no doubt are, but they too often seem to be a part of the storm instead of a part of the rescue. The possibility of being treated like a thing is quite as likely in the church at the corner as in the bank two blocks up the street.

The educators do not often make any public signs that they realize their fate. In spite of the prevailing nonrelational, non-Thou, noncommunicative experiences, they still can insist to one another that the church should preserve the sanctity of the person in his relationship with others.

Ross Snyder, a professor of Christian education and a more or less recognized leader in the field of relational education, has paraphrased a portion of Ephesians in a revealing fashion. Here we can perceive the mind and heart of modern Christian education throbbing out the good news about the person:

> The greatest picture of what a group is, comes in the letter to the Ephesians, as the writer attempts to state what has hap-pened to the Christians of the first century:
> "So then you are no longer strangers and sojourners"—

(*You are not alien, or "things" to each other.*)

"but you are fellow citizens with the saints and members of the household of God"—

(*There's a place for you within a people of God, and that fellowship is not limited just to the present people you face.*)

"built upon the foundation of the apostles and prophets, Christ Jesus himself being the chief cornerstone"—

(*You are growing out of the love and righteousness and redeeming that formed man, and makes all new.*)

"in whom the whole structure is joined together and grows into a holy temple in the Lord"—

(*You are members one of another, fitly joined together so that the corporateness can upbuild itself in love and each member grow toward maturity in Christ.*)

"in whom you also are built into it for a dwelling place of God in the Spirit."—

(*You are a presence to each other, and God's shaping purpose is present, in the togetherness.*)

This is what—in promise—every church school and church is.[10]

This is first-rate "Thou" talk, and at the same time bizarre exegesis, and an unacknowledged use of the ideas expounded principally by Harry Stack Sullivan. It is more or less symptomatic of the use that Christian educators have made of the findings of relational psychology, and that is where they have learned (or is it relearned?) that the person is a Thou who exists fundamentally in relationships, in meeting. Take away the Thou aspect of the person and you have the depersonalized person encountered by the droves every day. Add the Thou dimension and you have—instant Christian education.

The Person as Biblical Man

During the years 1930 to 1950 American theological seminaries offered courses in religious education and, later, Christian education, to essentially two kinds of students: the com-

---

[10] Ross Snyder, "Members One of Another . . . An Idea Whose Fulness of Time Has Come," *International Journal of Religious Education* (May, 1957), p. 8.

mitted and the skeptical. The committed were by and large
training themselves for professional work as religious (later,
Christian) educators in church schools, seminaries, or national
denominational boards of Christian education. The skeptical
looked down their noses at the very word "religious education."
They were training themselves either for the pastorate or for
professional teaching or Biblical scholarship. After the heady
intellectual activities in other seminary departments they found
the business of learning how to thread movie projectors boring
and the interminable group discussions so carefully moderated
by the professors a waste of time. Religious education was not
thought to be respectable, largely for the reason that it failed
to understand the Biblical faith or the Christian church. To
the skeptical, religious education seemed to belong more as an
arm to the public school than as an integral part of the church's
life.

Within the last ten years all that has changed. The seminary
Christian education departments have become more orthodox,
more Biblical, with a higher Christology, higher ecclesiology,
more definite third article of the creed than the Biblical or
systematic theology departments. "RE" courses can no longer
be safely taken as fluff courses. They go out of their way to
make the seminarian respect the substantial matters of faith
with which Christian education *now* deals.

A corresponding shift in the literature written by expert adult
educators can be perceived. One component of the new look,
especially as it concerns the much loved "person," startles the
unwary reader. This is, of course, the appearance of respectable
Biblical theology in large, well-ordered amounts. The experts
have discovered the neo-Reformation Biblical theology, which
means they have discovered God, the holy history, sin, Jesus
Christ, the Christian church, and the Holy Spirit. The educators
have what amounts to a compulsion to display their Biblical
credentials so that they will not be misunderstood or taken
lightly.

Let me cite an instance. Sara Little is a discerning adult
educator whose book *Learning Together in the Christian Fel-*

lowship was written for the use of laymen and has been widely circulated throughout adult education circles as a balanced, solid piece of work—which it surely is. Judge for yourself the import and intent of the following extract from her book:

Much that has been said about the mission of the church, and earlier, about God's purpose and plan for saving mankind, is relevant here. Several other thoughts may be helpful.

The whole history of God's dealing with man is a record of his working with the individual in community. There is a new awareness, these days, that salvation is not a transaction between one individual and God, carried on without relation to or concern for other people. Biblical scholars point out that a person's salvation comes to him, in part, as a member of a group; this is true in the New Testament as well as in the Old, for even here the individual is never thought of as being saved entirely by himself apart from the community of the saved.

God is the God of history. He does not detach himself from the world of men, waiting to be found by them; rather, he seeks them, confronting them in the midst of their experiences. The Bible is the drama of God at work in history, leading men in crisis and in everyday occurrences to interpret their experiences in the light of their faith. Thus he reveals himself. The creative interaction of men, struggling together to hear what God says in the events of today, becomes a medium by which he continues to confront them.

God's ultimate revelation is that of a Person speaking to persons. God incarnate in Jesus Christ, the "Word made flesh," spoke and speaks to man in act and in Being. Somehow, when a person meets Jesus Christ, all that he is and does speaks to other men of this Christ—and enables them to meet him, too. It is not one area of life that is touched, but the whole person. All that he is stands in awe before all that Christ is—and he is redeemed.

The Holy Spirit creates that kind of community in which the truth can be communicated. Men need feel no pride in their own accomplishment when it is evident that a truly redemptive community has come alive. This cannot happen without their full and free response to God's seeking love, it is true, but it is the Holy Spirit who creates real fellowship—*koinōnia*. Here it is that the "language of relationship, as well as the language of words, can exist." (A suitable quotation from the eminent relationalist Ross Snyder appropriately concludes the passage.)[11]

Miss Little's statements regarding Biblical theology are unexceptionable. She says the right things in the right way but in each instance for the purpose of driving the "thought" home, home being the group, the Christian fellowship, adult education and—the person. Thus, real exception can be taken to each conclusion she arrives at. Does God really confront men in their "creative interaction," i.e., their "struggling together to hear what God says in the events of today"? Does Miss Little know that much about God, or does she hope that God *might* confront men in (to use a less euphemistic term than creative interaction) study groups? Other portions of the Biblical record could be adduced by Miss Little to show the reluctance of the Biblical writers to assign any hopes at all to what God will do; yet these are not mentioned.

Similarly, she invokes the power of the blessed word "person" in order to connect incarnation with modern Christian education. Her second thought could as well have been stated in this way: "God's ultimate revelation is that of a Man speaking to men." The generic term "man" is more Biblical anyway, and were Paul seriously considered, we should have to use either "flesh" or "servant" in place of "man" or "person." She has used "person" as a style word, and it means in this context at least three things: individual, whole personality, man in league with the divine. And these are not irrelevant to her concerns in writing the book, one of which shows up in her third thought. There she denominates the relational syndrome of ideas (mysterious person meeting mysterious person in a Thou-ish sort of way) as the community that the Holy Spirit is interested in, indeed, that he creates.

Obviously, this particular educator has *not* merely thrown together some things that she has picked up from the Biblical

[11] Sara Little, *Learning Together in the Christian Fellowship* (John Knox Press, 1956), pp. 21, 22.

theologians in order to preserve a respectable front. She wrestles throughout her book with Biblical material in respect to the educational activities of the Christian fellowship. But she is committed to an appreciative view of the small group in the total Christian fellowship, and she equates Biblical man in covenant relation to Biblical God with modern persons confronting God in their mutual struggle.

Miss Little is not alone in making such an equation. Iris Cully, Randolph Crump Miller, and Lewis Sherrill—real heavyweights in the field—have attempted the same thing. Yet, their longer books, more replete with quotations, more exhaustive in development of Biblical themes, more Biblically fair and right, finally do no better than Sara Little has done in her less ambitious popular book. The major figures (and therefore the minor figures who follow them) have not wrestled with the possibility that the modern idea of person is not the same thing as Biblical *man*. Their description of the person has been formed by looking at the mature individual who comes off the analyst's couch essentially a new man, or they view with awe the wide-awake, alert, tolerant, free, open creature which they meet in group discussion labs. They tabulate their successes in deep personal relations with students or with laymen in the church. The person to them is an idealized portrait of all that modern man should be. Person rehearses for them all at once their educational aspirations. The educators want deep, lasting, significant education which occurs through deepening, lasting, significant relationships. But they do not test their image of the person against Biblical man. They do not submit their educational aspirations to the judgment of Scriptures; they find the Scriptures talking about just what they are talking about, namely, about a *koinōnia* that is sharp enough to arrange for small groups of persons to meet with the Holy Spirit in informal, democratically run discussion groups.

We have been going through some of the lore that surrounds

the word "person" in today's Christian education of adults. Because of its recent philosophical and theological antecedents we might have discovered that "person" meant a lonely Kierkegaardian individual, or an integrated Jungian personality, or perhaps the resplendent inner-directed man missed on American soil so keenly by David Reisman. But we have found a more gregarious creature given to sharing himself, relating himself, and meeting with others in the Christian fellowship, specifically in educational circumstances.

In the course of our investigations we have seen that the early alliance with general secular education has had something to do with the kind of person that Christian educators have come to reverence. But that does not tell the whole story. The person encountered in Christian education turns out to be a solid middle-class Protestant for whom meetings, talking, the formal paraphernalia of informality are understandable and typical. He does not relish being in a losing game. He likes his church to be successful and his education to be successful. The old-style Bible class didn't work, educationally. Bring on the new. Could *this* person actually be the average church member? By no means. In Chapter 1, our sobering analysis of local church groups revealed that no such desire for success can be documented. Who *is* the person, then? We might toy with the idea that he is the educator himself, for whom meetings, talking, the formal paraphernalia of informality are understandable and typical. I am getting around to saying that the stuff of the person, this person who relates and gives himself to to other persons, can be found in the educator himself. He furnishes the model as well as the description of the model. He happens to be a gregarious bureaucrat, for the most part. And a Christian education program that he finds acceptable, that he promotes—do not be surprised—features meetings, talking, sharing, and studied informality. This reverence for the person, therefore, might be seen as a form of self-reverence. That, at any rate, is an interesting theory which I, person-ally, happen to believe in. But this is crystal-clear: the persons appearing in the manuals bear little resemblance to the people in the churches or people in the Bible. And that fact should be taken seriously by anyone seriously interested in the local church variety of the Christian education of adults.

"Upon what basis shall the agency of formal education select the experiences that are to function in modifying adjustments?" . . .

This typical sentence illustrates a remarkable feature of the [new] language [Pedaguese], namely, its peculiar interchangeability of words. For instance, as we are assured by one of the most learned Pedaguese scholars in the United States, including Guam, the expression "experiences that are to function in modifying adjustments" means the same as the adjustments that are to modify in functioning experiences, or the functions that are to adjust in experiencing modifications, or the modifications that are to experience in adjusting functions. If you don't see the meaning of it in any form, read this:

"The fact that the organization of experience in coherent systems is a fundamental factor in promoting the application of experience to the practical improvement of adjustment is profoundly significant to the process of education." . . .

What is significant is that at first sight you may think this is English; but it isn't.[12]—*Welland Hendrich.*

[12] Welland Hendrich, *A Joysome History of Education* (A. G. Seiler, 1925), pp. 79, 80.

Chapter 3

ON THE CONCEPT

OF CHANGE

At a recent meeting of adult Sunday school teachers, I posed the following question, "Why do you teach?"

The fifteen teachers answered in various ways, but they had three basic answers, which were:

1. "I teach in order to make better disciples."

2. "I teach the Bible." (This was in each instance felt to be a self-explanatory answer.)

3. "I want to help people."

The answers presumed that:

1. The class members were not presently good enough disciples.

2. The class members did not know the Bible.

3. The class members needed help.

When the presumptions were stated that crassly to the teachers they began to qualify their original answers. One man allowed that he could not make better disciples, but he could be an instrument of the Holy Spirit. A woman teacher felt, on reflection, that the Bible teaches itself. The third group of teachers, however, held firm, feeling no need to refine or qualify their desire to help people.

My experience with these particular teachers could be duplicated with almost any fifteen teachers serving in any Protestant denomination. From curriculum materials they use, from the teacher-training events that they attend, from pastors and professional Christian educators with whom they consult, adult teachers have learned to think of themselves in these particular ways. Their work has something to do with helping people to be better Christians, and this work involves eventually the teaching of the Bible and inevitably involves in one way or another simply helping people to be simply better people. The present corps of teachers could have learned these goals from a previous generation of teachers, but the older generation learned the goals someplace.

The point is that the goals have been learned. In the long run, adult educators in the church are responsible for the goals. The typical teacher who meets a Sunday school class has a notion that he is going to change the class members. He may raise a demurrer about his prominence in the process of change and give major credit to the Holy Spirit, but he is nonetheless committed to goals and methods that are designed to change the learner from who he now is to a better person—in the eyes of the educators. The typical teacher is probably not overwhelmed by the evidence of change and secretly may be certain that *his* class members will never change, but the cumulative evidence of week after fruitless week, year after fruitless year, does little to alter his goals. Helpful change must be taking place because that is what should be happening. It may not be happening, but it should be, because change is the goal; therefore it probably is happening on such a deep level that the evidence in changed living has not yet appeared.

A few Christian educators of adults are beginning to have second thoughts about the goals of Christian education. The experience of little change happening has made them pessimistic, if not cynical, about the goal of change itself. These educators are far ahead of typical educators and teachers who still think in terms of change. Probably the major reason why no change, or very little change, does take place is that change has been adopted as a goal of education.

It is, of course, a respectable goal. Secular educators would be lost without it. To secular adult education, change is the stuff of the educational process. These educators believe their educational methods to be tools by which a job is accomplished, that job being teaching a skill, reorienting thought, shifting attitudes, or communicating a body of knowledge in such a way that the learner becomes more aware of himself, his community problems, and so on. In each instance the learner changes. He becomes a different person to the extent that he, for instance, acquires a new reading skill. The educators believe, many of them passionately, that an adult with reading skill is a better adult than the unskilled reader. The skilled reader reads more and better material, and the more he reads the better citizen he is bound to become.

A secular adult educator, writing for the *International Journal of Religious Education,* uses the word "change" in a revealing way:

What, then, are the proper objectives of education, and which method is best fitted to each? The following list of objectives and methods suitable to them is based on a system of categories developed by Ralph Tyler, director of the Center for the Advanced Study of the Behavioral Studies:

Changes in things known, or knowledge: lecture, reading, audio-visual aids, question and answer, forum, symposium.

Changes in things comprehended, or understanding: problem-solving projects, discussion, laboratory experiments, demonstration, role-playing, panels.

Changes in things done, or skills: demonstration, practice drill, apprenticeship.

Changes in things felt, or attitudes: successful experience with a new attitude (role-playing, field trip, permissive discussion, counseling).

Changes in things valued, or appreciation: inspirational talk, discussion, reading, films, visits.

Changes in things liked, or interest: exposure to new interests, starting with present interests (discussion, reading, audio-visual aids, field trips).

In planning a particular learning activity, it will of course be necessary to spell out the specific knowledge, understanding, skill, attitude, appreciation, or interest related to each objective. And it is important to recognize that more than one type of objective may be achieved in a single activity. For example, knowledge is seldom useful without understanding; therefore it is usually desirable to combine a lecture with discussion or some other method in which learners practice using their knowledge.[13]

A change, according to this representative list of desirable objectives, is a shift, a movement from one place to another, often a giving up of one position in favor of a better position; or change may be movement in a growth process from less to more mature, no matter how significant or insignificant the specific movement is. We might also note that not all kinds of change are subject to accurate measurement or, in a few cases, to any documentation. A change in appreciation or attitude can happen without anyone else's knowing about it. Thus the goals, properly yoked to suitable methods, might well be realized without the educator's being aware that he has had any success. However, such unmeasurable changes are unlikely. An attitude does eventually show, after all, and will display itself in one way or another.

By making such a list, Malcolm Knowles has said simply what other educators, in and out of the church, have been saying in more complicated, and often, elevated language. *Educators want, plan for, and achieve desirable changes in the learner or they get out of the business.* That, plainly, is what education is all about. Learning is change. Stated in its negative form the thesis reads: without change there is no learning. Christian educators accept that thesis, and so we have adult education in the church aiming at the changed individual and devising suitable methods to produce the desirable changes.

An Illustration
Racial Prejudice
A Project in Education

A pastor in a Northern city becomes concerned over a po-

---

[13] Malcolm Knowles, "Use Effective Methods," *International Journal of Religious Education* (May, 1959), p. 14.

tentially dangerous situation developing in his parish. Negroes
have been attempting to buy property in the parish, so far
without success, but with an aggressiveness that to his parishioners is sinister. His parishioners are white. They think of
themselves as enlightened folk and speak to one another as if
they had no vestiges of what in a less liberal community might
be called prejudice. Their consternation at the possibility of
interracial neighborhoods in *their* community is a clear enough
indication that they have not fully overcome their prejudices
or at least their prejudice that they would rather have money
than lose it. For this is the specific content of their consternation: they feel that property values deteriorate in an interracial community; they own property; therefore, an interracial
community means that they lose money.

The pastor knows already that preaching even a long series
of sermons will not touch the situation. He also knows that
action by the church's official body will not change many
minds. How, then, can he change the minds of his people?
What can he do and—to him a more important question—
what *should* he do? He could try to educate the educatable
and hope for the best. He has massive support from the professional educators of his denomination. He thus sends for
suitable materials, makes his plans, and begins his project in
adult education, a project, by the way, that has much at stake
and is not to be thought of as a time filler, a bit of religious
busy work, or an "experiment in human relations."

The pastor tries first of all to cool off the potential hysteria
that has been brewing. So he conceives of a number of public,
all-congregational meetings at which he will try to present the
following facts in a favorable light.

1. Property values do not deteriorate in an interracial neighborhood *if* residents do not sell their property.

2. Property values do deteriorate when residents become
frightened and offer their property for sale in panic.

3. A neighborhood remains stable if stable residents attempt
to include rather than reject new neighbors.

These facts are made available through the use of a movie,
a forum, and the distribution of attractive and down-to-earth

pamphlets. The people who attend, a disappointingly small percentage of the total congregation, have ample opportunity to voice their fears, argue over the facts, present new "facts" in support of the idea that property values go down *no matter what,* and socialize in an unusual setting. The results are disappointing. The potential hysteria has not materially altered. People now do not talk to one another as readily as they once talked, because the facts have been made public, and the facts do not agree with private opinion.

Stage two of this project gets under way by the establishment of numerous cottage meeting groups at which, in more intimate, informal settings, people may be given the opportunity to grapple more directly with their prejudices. The pastor uses a number of devices in these cottage meetings. He uses role-playing, for instance, in skillful ways. At one meeting he has the most volubly prejudiced person assume the role of a Negro doctor who is talking for the first time with the white couple who live next door. Another meeting gives the pastor the chance to introduce to the folks who have indirectly turned him down as a potential neighbor a role-played Negro who has attempted unsuccessfully to buy a house in the community. In other meetings the pastor allows the people to talk—just talk—in the hope that they will gain some insight into the nature and mechanisms of their prejudice.

With the official board of the church the pastor initiates a program of intensive study. He lays before the board some theological materials prepared by the denomination and urges a mature, reflective study of what a church is and what its mission is in situations of rapid social change. He also begins an unofficial Bible-study group whose announced purpose is to grapple with the Biblical understanding of "man's obligation to man." These study situations, he plans, will eventually produce church members with insight and courage. And on these members he places his major hopes. If serious study of the Biblical and theological heritage of the church cannot illuminate the demands of the community situation, then, reasons the pastor, the demands will not ever be understood.

He therefore throws himself into these activities hopefully and with conviction, realizing that the church stands or falls with the church's students—the official board and the eleven volunteer members of the Bible-study group.

After six weeks of study the pastor begins to feel that his students have no capacity to relate the insights found in study materials to the concrete community situation. The pastor consistently provokes discussion of the community situation and leads abstract study to practical issues but, he learns, his efforts are fruitless. He finds that the students have branded him a likable zealot. They identify every threatening insight with his radicalism. He, John Calvin, and the Bible become for the students a single voice that has no force or relevance. They have avoided change while preserving amicable relationships with the pastor, who is, at this point, defeated. His project, launched with rare courage and conducted with resourcefulness and skill, has not succeeded, because his people plainly have not budged. They remain perdurably hostile to the idea of an interracial community in spite of his best, most friendly, attempts to lead them out of their cruel bigotry into the openness of personal freedom.

This illustration—a fictional compound of elements from many "true" stories—has no happy ending, because education is not equipped to do that kind of job. Yet, according to Christian educators, precisely that kind of job can be done. Adult education is designed to facilitate change in people. Give them the opportunity, provide suitable motivation, proper resources, and skilled leadership, and they *will* change. This is the open-ended promise made by Christian educators. The pastor in the illustration believed the promise and sought with every tool available to him to make the promise come true. But the desired and desirable changes did not occur. Such a notable failure dramatizes the numerous failures of other pastors, adult leaders, and adult teachers who have exercised neither his skill nor passion in projects that have in comparison mattered very little. And failures lead us to question the promise itself, to scrutinize the apparatus of theory undergirding the promise, and to ask what sense we can make out of the category of change itself as the central methodological concern of adult education.

Change is basically a spatial idea. A body "changes" direction, which means that the forces propelling it in one direction are altered in such a way that the body moves in a different direction. This change in direction can be simple or complex, but it is at all events a genuine, i.e., observable, change. A body likewise can change shape through the operation of exterior altering forces. It can be split into two pieces, or dented, or added to so that it becomes a bigger body. Its appearance can be altered by the application of paint or by oxidation. It can be acted upon in such a way that it is changed. To the physical scientist change is an excellent descriptive category. It is meaningful to him as he describes, foresees, constructs, and at times apprehends bodies in motion.

Change, however, is not so useful in describing temporal process. Time does not change. The time of day does not change; time goes on; it endures; it sweeps; its movement from future into present into past is inexorable, precisely unchangeable. The course of a man's life from his birth is fixed toward his encroaching death and cannot detour to the side, stop, or move backward. His life flows ever onward in one direction: into the future with an often frighteningly implacable step. Thus, to say that a person has changed from infancy to boyhood to youth to manhood employs the word "change" in a fruitless manner. *When* did he change? At what second did he cross the line from youth into adulthood? At what fraction of a second, to be precise? Obviously no such precision is possible in dating these so-called changes, and for that reason the word is useless in such a context. Time is more dramatically—and accurately—defined as the press of the future into a brief present as it slips into an irretrievable past.

Psychologically change has little use because it is imprecise. In the laboratory a change can be measured. A liquid is 42 degrees centigrade. A ball bounces 5.54 feet. A bullet is deflected at an angle of 24 degrees. A hydrogen electron moves at the speed of 1,300 miles per hour. But how can an emotional change be measured? No devices are conceivable to measure the weight, size, color, or speed of hostility, and the fact that a person who carries hostile emotions becomes less hostile cannot be reckoned on a scale. Thus, of what possible use is the word "change"? The hostile person is not as hostile as he once was. That is a statement of fact. The person has not "changed"; nor have his emotions changed. Something dramatically inward has happened to vitiate the intensity of certain emotions, therefore allowing other emotions more free expression.

As a matter of course psychologists and psychiatrists do speak of change, but the word as they use it has a metaphorical quality. It does not denote measurability but eventfulness. A personality change has the character of a happening, and that happening can be described in terms of personal decision, struggle, suffering, integrity, and commitment. The events that are spoken of as producing the change have to do with the subtle exercise of the will, the opening of the person to new experiences, to risks, to suffering, and so on. The word "change," therefore, when used psychologically, bears an accent of tentativeness, of apprehensiveness, and even of mysteriousness.

Now, what usefulness has the word "change" when used theologically? A Christian educator says:

> Christian education is the attempt, ordinarily by members of the Christian community, to participate in and to guide the changes which take place in persons in their relationships with God, with the church, with other persons, with the physical world and with oneself.[14]

What *precisely* does he mean by the word "change"? There simply is no precise answer. The particular educator whom we

[14] Lewis J. Sherrill, *The Gift of Power* (The Macmillan Company, 1955), p. 82.

have quoted seems to understand a changed relationship as a deepened relationship, a qualitatively different relationship, or as he argues in other places, a "new" relationship. "Change" for him describes the remarkable differences that personalities undergo in relationships. The sullen, underdeveloped, suspicious person in a relationship of trust undergoes altogether startling transformations. He becomes himself trusting, generous, settled, and seems to develop potentialities toward life fullness.

Likewise, persons who actually have quite mature life views and in the main have found satisfactory solutions to life problems have inexplicably immature religious ideas. These people, when guided by the Christian community to participate in the study of the Scriptures and the theological traditions of their religious heritage, grow up intellectually in the religious sphere. Their ideas change, but the use of the word "change" points in the direction of replacement. Traditional ideas, once lightly held and ill-considered, when exposed to examination, are discarded or deepened but at all events replaced by substantially more mature ideas. Again, the idea of change can be seen to point to a more specific idea, in this case, replacement and deepening. The person's ideas have not actually changed but have been discarded, and new ideas have taken their place. The person willing these inward intellectual activities has not changed. He has different ideas about his Christian faith, and that, in its barest, minimal statement is the only accurate description of the matter.

Theoretical statements of the aims of adult education prominently display the word "change," and no amount of sympathetic analysis of what lies behind the use of the word "change" can take away the presupposed view of the learner and of the teacher.

The learner, when looked upon as the person who is to undergo suitable changes, is basically viewed in the objective case by the changer. The learner is the acted-upon, the receiver of new information, the holder of certain soon-to-be-changed ideas. He is frankly a very sophisticated and unpredictable object who does not conform to Newton's laws of motion but who nonetheless can and does change under proper conditions. Adult educators consider capacity for a change an axiom on which the structure of adult education is based. Thus the picture of the learner corresponds surprisingly to the picture of an object in the laboratory of the physical scientist.

Consider the situation described earlier in the chapter. The pastor (teacher) sought to provoke changes in the members of the congregation. The pastor would find widespread theological support for his views about the desirability of integrated community life. The desirability of his goals does not at this point have much material bearing on his lack of success. Concretely, how did he conceive of the members of the congregation—the "learners"? His specific emotions about them may have had a final bearing on his lack of success, and some educators would feel *the* final bearing. He perhaps disliked them in disagreeing with them, undoubtedly was hostile toward their reluctance to change, or exhibited the scorn of a recent convert toward the unbeliever. These emotions, if present, no doubt did inhibit his total effectiveness. But, though worthy of mention, the pastor's emotions did not finally jeopardize the success of a project that displays by its singular arrangement the marks of incipient defeat. The learners were conceived of as *change objects*. That in itself was the central force inhibiting the desired change. And the people in that congregation were much too alive to be properly conceived of as mere change objects.

People are not change objects. People do not change. They act and react. They are forced either to adopt new ideas by pressures brought to bear on them in their life situation, or else to resist these pressures with unmeasured willfulness. Metaphorically speaking, people *are changed* when life breaks in on them, when the future suddenly opens up and provokes decision. The adults who ignored the educational attempts of their pastor willed not to be changed. They stubbornly and resourcefully resisted change. Their minds remained full of their own ideas. Their wills continued to direct them stead-fastly in a course that no amount of educational training—of the mind or of the feelings—could possibly alter. That was the trouble. The people willed not to learn and the pastor was helpless before their stubbornness. A thousand hours of study failed to produce what one Negro neighbor could have produced in one week.

The learner, when viewed as a change object, reacts as a willful human being. Some learners, already committed to wanting to learn, do learn; they replace some ideas with better ones; their openness to new ideas predisposes them to welcome new ideas; their thirst for reliable information is slaked only by reliable information; a profound shift deep within them leads them to accept new—often radical—social change. Learning of the nature described in Christian education man-uals *does occur* but *only* in individual learners, who act sur-prisingly unlike change objects because they have disposed themselves to learn before they enter the Christian education situation. The situation that seeks to change them is incapable of changing them and can operate successfully only with those who have undergone so-called changes outside the situation. Observable attitude shifts occur in those people who *unob-servably* face toward their future and away from their past.

The viewer-of-the-learner as a change object is the "change force" or the director of the change forces, i.e., the educator himself. He should never be upstaged by the learner in this analysis, because he figures more prominently in the produc-tion of desirable change than does the change object.

Consider once more the pastor in the unsuccessful educa-tional venture we have described. His own estimate of himself was, of course, fully at work throughout his attempts to edu-cate the congregation. But in choosing the methods that he did to effect the changes he sought, he also chose a role that fitted the methods he selected. He was the self-conscious changer. Among many prejudiced people, he acted as the force to change prejudice. The people were immediately and constantly aware of his role. Having more wisdom than change objects are credited with possessing, the people rejected his role while maintaining friendship with him as a pastor, man, fellow human being, and so on. Yet, in the face of this rejection he continued his resourceful but nonetheless unavailing operations. He ordered the films and planned the time for showing them. He was the author or immediate source of the educational materials. He initiated discussion; he led the study. At every point where he portrayed himself as the antagonist to their ideas he was dismissed as easily as the learners dismissed John Calvin or the Bible.

Had the pastor been more sophisticated in his method, he would never have exposed himself as the change force. He would have enlisted other people in a committee arrangement, thus deflecting suspicion away from himself onto the committee at large. But that would not have altered the suspicion. Each committeeman or person selected by the committee to exercise leadership of any nature would have experienced that rejection reserved in the concrete situation for the pastor, who did not, recall, have the favorably inclined personnel with which to establish a committee. No matter who operates as the change agent or applies the pressure to change, he receives in his role the force of rejection by people who refuse to conform to their unwanted role as change objects.

In adopting his role as change agent, the pastor participated in an educational venture that could, with more accuracy, be described as a rigged game. The learner has got to come out at a different place. The goal of the "venture" is not change in general but a specified change. No one would coldly set up the problem in just this way, but, coldly, this is exactly what it amounts to: One man undertook to change the minds of many other people. He got it into his head that what was in their heads was wrong and needed changing. He could be successful, and within his definition of success, the other people could be successful only if *he* changed *them*. No matter how much was at stake—and, remember, in a real sense the future of the community was at stake—the venture itself was doomed to failure because it was educational, because change was the admitted goal, because one man acted as change agent, because the other people were considered as, but refused to act as, change objects.

This single situation has now probably been overanalyzed. Let it stand for the Sunday morning Bible class, the adult class using denominational curriculum materials, the informal study group, the official board of a local church, a couples group, a group of women or men, a teachers' meeting, or a congregational meeting. In any one of these situations the theoretical understanding of the Christian education of adults supplied by professional Christian educators proves inadequate and inappropriate to the situation. If learning is change in the individual, and Christian education the means for stimulating these changes, then little learning is taking place in the church today. And the reasons for the failure of the Christian education of adults in these situations can be found in the situation described at some length above.

Change cannot be the central methodological concern of adult education, no matter how desirable the changes contemplated may be. A fatal misunderstanding of the human situation mars the theory. Man is not a being subject to change. He remains man amidst the flux of circumstances, standing unalterably in his history, committed to a life view with such conviction that competitors—especially serious competitors—cannot be acknowledged, much less considered. Man from the inside of himself sees life in his own terms and is adept at protecting the sanctity of his unchallengeable solitude. He is fundamentally a willful being, not an intellectual or an emotional being, and any theory that does not reckon on the strength of that will must eventually flounder on hard facts or can at best enjoy a minimal success because of the kindly predisposition of the learner's will.

Although the Bible has occupied the attentions and concerns of adult education throughout its brief history and Biblical theology in the past twenty years has gained significant stature among Christian educators, one of the fundamental motifs of Biblical thought has been largely overlooked, namely, the primacy of the will. The project of wedding the Biblical faith to sound educational theory—a project undertaken generally by Christian educators throughout Protestantism—thus has been dominated by a view of man provided by the secular educational theorists, with consequences that are just now beginning to emerge. The course of life itself—rather, the courses of the lives of the educators—has demonstrated the truth of the Biblical insistence on the stubbornness of man's will and has thrown suspicion on the somewhat vain opinion held among educators that adults are capable of provoked change.

Present educational theory should not, probably, be called Pelagian, because it has not been formulated as was the thought of Pelagius, in sharp conflict with an Augustinian statement of the bondage of the will. But it does sound Pelagian and at that point deserves some of the criticism accorded to that position in the history of Christian thought. Pelagius argued, on—to him—unshakable grounds, that man is capable of responding to the preachments of the gospel, or else they never would have been written and preserved. Man can will to will the will of God. He can appropriate to himself the goodness of atonement. The form of Pelagius' statement of man's capacities has, of course, been determined by the form of Augustine's classic restatement of Paul's position on the bondage and corruption of the will. But, nevertheless, Pelagius has put into convenient form a long-standing optimistic portrait of man that has been reproduced in large part by modern Christian educators of adults. They hold with Pelagius that man fundamentally tends to want to respond, to be educated, to learn. He enjoys a rapport with the creation that prompts him to appropriate to himself goodness. Through training he can better himself, better his thinking equipment, *and* his will.

Well, this was the whole point in the original dispute between Pelagius and Augustine and is the central point to be raised with contemporary theories of adult education. Is man, after all, susceptible to education—of his will? Modern educators claim that learning goes hand in hand with deep character changes, and they aim for these changes. The Pauline-Augustinian position furnishes a robust "No" to the question. Man is not a bad or a good being. But man is an enslaved being—in bondage to evil or to God, incapable of extricating himself from his fateful imprisonment. He cannot break the bars of his prison by the exercise of his will. He is a wretched man, who is not only incapable of doing the good deeds that his will tells him to will but who cannot overcome his remorse over his failure. Man's will, according to Paul and Augustine, has been captured. This is why a modern exegete of Paul can claim that education in modern terms is impossible. The mind may be apprised of stimulating new information, the emotions directed toward desirable and attractive objects, but the will that directs the man—*IS the man* —steers in a contrary direction, guiding the mind and the emotions in a life course that, destructive, benign, complacent, or successful, cannot be changed except by the will itself.

Exasperating modern testimony to the profound truth of this Pauline-Augustinian position can be found in abundance, probably none more vivid than the case of Ellen West, written by the existential psychiatrist Ludwig Binswanger. Wellborn, well cared for, intelligent, vital, Ellen West became progressively dominated by intolerable anxiety over eating. As this domination exercised itself, the walls of her future narrowed correspondingly until there was literally no further place to go. She then committed suicide. Two extracts from her writing that have been preserved in the case history furnish compelling insight into the life of this young woman. She writes:

> The murderer must feel somewhat as I do who constantly sees in his mind's eye the picture of the victim. He can work, even slave, from early until late, can go out, can talk, can attempt to divert himself: all in vain. Always and always again he will see the picture of the victim before him. He feels an overpowering pull toward the place of the murder. He knows that this makes him suspect. Even worse—he has a horror of that place, but still

he must go there. Something that is stronger than his reason and his will controls him and makes of his life a frightful scene of devastation. The murderer can find redemption. He goes to the police and accuses himself. In the punishment he atones for his crime. I can find no redemption—except in death.

I continue living only because of a sense of duty to my relatives. Life has no further lure for me. There is nothing, no matter where I look, which holds me. Everything is gray and without joy. Since I have buried myself in myself, and can no longer love, existence is only torture. Every hour is torture. What formerly gave me joy is now a task, an intrinsically senseless something contrived to help me pass the hours. What formerly seemed to me a goal in life, all the learning, all the striving, all the accomplishment, is now a dark, heavy nightmare of which I am afraid.

Ask a prisoner of war sometime whether he would rather stay in the prison camp or return to his homeland. In the prison camp he studies foreign languages and concerns himself with this or that: of course, only to help himself get over the long, hard days. Does he really enjoy the work? Would he for its sake remain in the prison camp even a minute longer than necessary? Certainly not, and nobody would even dream up such a grotesque idea. But of me it is required. Life has become a prison camp for me, and I long as ardently for death as the poor soldier in Siberia longs for his homeland.

The comparison with imprisonment is no play on words. I am in prison, caught in a net from which I cannot free myself. I am a prisoner within myself: I get more and more entangled, and every day is a new, useless struggle; the meshes tighten more and more. I am in Siberia; my heart is icebound; all around me is solitude and cold. My best days are a sadly comic attempt to deceive myself as to my true condition. It is undignified to live on like this. Karl, if you love me, grant me death. . . . I am surrounded by enemies. Wherever I turn, a man stands there with drawn sword. As on the stage: The unhappy one rushes toward the exit; stop! an armed man confronts him. He rushes to a second, to a third exit. All in vain. He is surrounded, he can no longer get out. He collapses in despair.

So it is with me: I am in prison and cannot get out. It does no good for the analyst to tell me that I myself place the armed men there, that they are theatrical figments and not real. *To me they are very real.*

The entire world-picture is disarranged. As if I were be-witched. An evil spirit accompanies me and embitters my joy in everything. He distorts everything beautiful, everything natural, everything simple, and makes a caricature out of it. He makes a caricature out of all life. . . .

Something in me rebels against becoming fat. Rebels against becoming healthy, getting plump red cheeks, becoming a simple, robust woman, as corresponds to my true nature. . . . It drives me to despair that with all my big words I cannot get myself further. I am fighting against uncanny powers which are stronger than I. I cannot seize and grasp them.[15]

Ellen West was, of course, a sick woman, and I cannot possibly use her to represent mankind or even a segment of mankind. She represents herself alone, and that inadequately. Her remarks about her condition are cited, however, on the theological hunch that her words could be taken as auto-biographical by a great many people who would probably be astonished to discover another person articulating so clearly their own interior condition. This hunch has been experi-mentally validated with remarkably positive results.

Personal life proceeds on a course that simply is not altered by educational projects, and in such a way that the educational projects appear irrelevant at best and oppressive at the worst to the person. The future alone has the power to change the course of personal life and even then can exercise its power only under conditions guaranteed by a person who is open to his future and willing to be made willing to accept with grati-tude the grace with which God has filled the future.

A largely Pelagian educational theory, dominated by a methodological concern for change, does not reckon seriously with the willful resistance of the learner to the educator and for that reason fails at the point it most desires to succeed.

[15] Ludwig Binswanger, in *Existence, A New Dimension in Psychiatry and Psychology*, edited by Rollo May, Ernest Angel, and Henri F. Ellenberger (Basic Books, Inc., 1958), pp. 256–259.

A man and his will are identical. If his will is in bondage to evil, which is what the New Testament always assumes, the whole man is in bondage to evil. He cannot therefore dissociate himself from his will, or summon it back from evil. In Rom. 7:15–25, Paul unfolds the contradiction between what a man wills and what he actually does—"what I would, that I do not; but what I have, that do I." Here the will which wills the "good" is not man's empirical will, but the basic impulse which lies behind all actual acts of the will, the desire for life as something that is good. If this basic impulse is incapable of realization, it means that the empirical will cannot will what it really wills. Consequently, education or training of the will is useless. What is needed is to bring home to the will its utter impotence: so that it can cry: "O wretched man that I am! Who shall deliver me from the body of this death?"[16]—*Rudolf Bultmann.*

[16] Rudolf Bultmann, *Primitive Christianity in Its Contemporary Setting* (Living Age Books, Meridian Books, Inc., 1956), p. 181.

Chapter *4*

BIBLICAL IGNORANCE

In the foregoing analysis I have been intent on pointing out certain structural weaknesses in the theory and practice of the Christian education of adults. Ordinarily the practice in a particular church lags painfully behind the advanced suggestions proposed by denominational specialists. But were that lag to be overcome, and in a few churches it has been, there would still exist a gulf between the goals and the accomplishments of the program. To some extent the goals have been poorly, naïvely, or unrealistically conceived. Furthermore, the theories themselves seem to incapacitate, indeed, to *scuttle* the possibilities for reaching the goals. Specifically, the educational project conceiving the "learner" as a "person" having "real needs" who can "learn" only if those "real needs" are "being met," and which "learning" is to be thought of as a specifiable "change" or series of "changes" has within it the seeds of failure. The learners conspire unconsciously in sabotage, acting in willfully obstructive ways. This phenomenon, documented by teachers and leaders—both pastors and laymen—throughout the church, spells frustration for the educators who have hoped for too much and an occasion for wistful evasion of the facts by those educators who have stubbornly refused to give up their hopes.

Undoubtedly the central difficulty to be discovered in the

75

theory and practice of the Christian education of adults is the use of the adjective "Christian." Therein lies the ambiguity that is seldom recognized and when recognized, unsatisfactorily dealt with.

Does Christian education refer to a distinctive kind of education that differs so remarkably from other kinds of education that it can accurately be called Christian?

Or, is the Christian education of adults the education of Christians—using methods, procedures, and purposes that do not especially differ from those of general, secular education?

Or, are the education and the educated uniquely Christian?

The literature dealing with the theory of Christian education, as well as the program and curriculum materials supplied by denominations, avoids the issues at stake by resorting to a high doctrine of the church. By Christian education of adults is meant, for all practical working purposes, *the churchly education of churchmen*. A certain wisdom can be found in such an evasion, a wisdom learned from John Calvin, who hesitated, with his doctrine of the visible and invisible church, to identify the true saints and therefore operated on the assumption that communicating, baptized members of the church are Christians. But this wisdom acknowledged, the evasion must be faced for what it is, because this evasion is ultimately responsible for many of the church's dilemmas and for much of the ineffectual education that is being conducted by the church.

Church school classes and informal study groups are filled with adults who refuse to learn, who resist change. For that reason they cannot be fairly represented in any real New Testament sense as being members of the eschatological body of Christ; i.e., they are not open to their future of grace, i.e., they are not Christians. And, apparently, gaining that future of grace is not a prospect to which they look forward. A future of grace is not *gained*, no matter if actively pursued. It cannot be bought at the A & P, engineered by subtle operators of group pressures, cunningly arranged for by dedicated churchmen, prepared for, or imagined. That which *is* most needful can only be received as a gift from God. Only God can turn the will around in its life course. The fruitless activities of the educators, as well as the resistance of the learners, constantly demonstrate the futility of attempts to accomplish what is not in the province of adult education to effect. Carelessly using the Greek word *koinōnia* to describe study groups, recklessly hailing libidinous warmth as "redemptive forces," does not create *koinōnia* within study groups or transmute veiled sexuality into redemption.

The fundamental precondition of *Christian* education must be the presence of Christians who, prompted by the Spirit, speak to each other about the graciousness of God and exhibit through mutual confession and exhortation their ultimate loyalty to Jesus Christ as Lord. Without the presence of the Spirit such speech becomes conversation, but in the Spirit it is the word of God. The foolishness of speaking (preaching) about Jesus Christ, according to Paul, lies in its tentativeness. The Spirit provides the eyes with which to see Jesus as the Christ and the ears with which to hear words about Jesus as the Word of God. The eyes and ears of faith are strictly the creation of God. Without them the gospel appears to the listener as an interesting story, a blasphemous lie, bad news, a judgment, or almost anything—but not, definitely *not,* good news about God.

Willingness to be given the gracious Word of God calls fundamentally for a converted will. And this transformed, more nearly re-formed, will has its essential course in life altered. It now causes the Christian man to listen for the Word of God with the ears of faith fashioned by the Spirit, and it leads the Christian man to behold with eyes of faith the work of God in the imminent future. Thus Paul. He was persistently running into a future that was designated on its ultimate edge as the Parousia and in its next moment as a splendid, undeserved gift. Shipwrecks, imprisonments, stonings, hunger, and rebuff held no terror for him; they were occasions for reveling in God's goodness.

Previous to his conversion the contents of Paul's *past* exercised a normative and fascinating importance for his life. He was oriented to Rome, the Torah, his teacher Gamaliel, and the tribe of Benjamin. Within this orientation he found it inconceivable that the Christian gospel might be true. He therefore energetically went about stamping out the heresy. After his conversion Paul found his life oriented around what was *going to happen*. Not even the superlatively historical events of Jesus' crucifixion and resurrection were merely "past" events around which he might arrange his life. He *daily* was crucified with Christ. He lived *in* the reality of a *continual* resurrection. In this incredible fashion the contents of the good news that are essential testamonia concerning what God *has* done came streaming in on Paul out of the future, tokens of God's favor, newly delivered gifts from the hand of a prodigally lavish God.

The Christian man, according to this brief analysis of Paul's thought, can speak about Jesus Christ to another Christian and only then be understood, both speaker and listener readily and joyously acknowledging that the power of this speech is God's doing. Moreover, the speaking, as Word of God, has a decisive quality. It comes out of the future: it is filled with surprise, suddenness, shock, and inspires awe, insight, and faith. This speech is authentic preaching, performed within the community of saints for edification and instruction. Its purpose is to ready the saints for what God is doing and is about to do. By the Word of God, the saints are turned from a conformation to the world, which is oriented about dependable experience— validated and centered on visible structures of order and power —to participation in the life of the Spirit, wherein all things are made continually new, i.e., have *never before happened*. Paul's central affirmation is: "We have received not the spirit of the world, but the Spirit which is from God, that we might understand the gifts bestowed on us by God" (I Cor. 2:12). The stance of the Christian man in the Christian community is light-footed; he leans expectantly toward the eventfulness of what has not yet happened but what will bear for him unimaginable consequences. There, in the "not yet," he continually confronts the grace of his King Jesus.

Accordingly, Christian education that does not constantly presuppose speaking about the active, soon to come, now, *happening* grace of God has not rightly used the adjective "Christian" and has in using it supplied a content gained not from the frontier on which the future becomes "now" but, rather, from the past, the "then," from what experience has taught, events have made certain, common sense dictates, educational theory postulates, etc. Christian educators may allude to the churchman, the educatee, as a Christian, and may—though not necessarily—mean a person whose will has been re-formed, but this radically important designation is not the sort of thing that can be alluded to in such a fashion that it is taken for granted, or treated as if it needed only scant reference. In hinting that conversion is a more or less pious, subjective experience that not all Christians have been through, and for *that* reason refusing to give much space to the subject, Christian educators have perforce committed themselves to a theoretical program of Christian education that no longer has any reason for being called "Christian" and might with greater candor be termed simply churchcraft.

To be fair, we must recognize that the educational literature supplied to local churches does not explicitly announce itself as being churchly education. Much of its content concerns Biblical materials, Christian thought, issues facing modern Christians, missionary activity. The publishers of the material make clean, evangelical statements of purpose, affirming the Lordship of Jesus Christ and a laudable aim of providing opportunities for Christians to become more knowledgeable, better disciples. There is abundant talk about Jesus Christ. Gospel records are studied at great length. Old Testament studies are often undertaken. And it should be noted that seldom is the Biblical faith treated as information. The educational specialists who prepare the materials are responsible and often theologically learned people. They admit to high purposes and propose goals of great splendor—if little realism.

But one fact rises to predominant importance for our considerations. These materials are *educational*. They are prepared for study and discussion in contrived, formal circumstances. What can the specialists do at this point? They are hired by a denomination to prepare educational materials *for* that denomination. The denomination devises means to interest local churches in using the materials. The local churches in turn find ways to engage individual church members in educational activities making use of the materials. Educational programs are primarily and necessarily exercises in churchcraft. Many of the specialists are cynical about the probability, but they must presume, professionally at least, that churchmen who use the materials are Christians. On this point the enterprise of Christian education flounders and becomes, as we have said, churchly education. The material—of whatever character, including that of the Bible—comes into a situation that more often than not reckons successful education in terms of the number of members present, or, in more sophisticated groups, the number of discussants who made meaningful contributions. Furthermore, the supporting material offered to educational leaders regularly moves past matters of substance in order to help the leader to determine his pedagogical strategy, as if, by tacit mutual agreement, matters of substance will take care of themselves, while such matters as successful sessions cannot be left to chance or whimsey.

Although adult educators in the church have made some disastrous theoretical mistakes in conceiving goals and procedures, adult education suffers fundamentally from a deeper, more sinister malaise. The people who participate in the educational ventures as teachers and as learners have breathed the air of a church-centered pietism that seems to be peculiarly American and that certainly spells nothing but trouble for any kind of education. That mythical average Protestant owns ideas about church, Bible, and life in general that are antagonistic, structurally, to a future of grace. These ideas can be identified indirectly through the songs that appeal to him, the political candidates he votes for, the movies he approves of, his choice of a wife (or husband), the alacrity with which he gives rousing sanction to other religions of international repute and is defiantly intolerant of Roman Catholic Christians in his local neighborhood.

The problems encountered by adult education are chiefly found in an ecclesiastical mind-set whose very amorphousness is significant. The typical Protestant enjoyed the blasphemous movie *The Ten Commandments*, but denounced the beautifully acted, skillfully moral *Room at the Top*. His American Protestant tradition led him unerringly to both decisions. A movie about the Bible is good. A movie about adultery is bad.

A melodramatic series of books by and about an enthusiastic user of theatrical metaphors, Peter Marshall, sold impressively to an enthusiastic reading public that was appalled by a passably good movie production of Sinclair Lewis' scathing *Elmer Gantry*.

Will Herberg in *Protestant-Catholic-Jew* and Martin Marty in *The New Shape of American Religion* produce massive amounts of incontrovertible evidence that the typical Protestant is interested at best in religion-in-general but shies at the authentic cadences of Biblical faith. This Protestant participates in educational ventures sponsored by the church. He is "the adult" of adult education. Symbolically speaking, Mr. Protestant sits comfortably under the Sallman *Head of Christ* as he is getting his Christian education and, more often than not, is warmly responsive to that picture, which has been called many things, perhaps none as true to the mark as "The All-American Boy."

For this typical Protestant, Jesus Christ is encountered as a heroic figure of the past who performed unusual miracles and was thus the Son of God. Jesus Christ is a romantic figure of leonine proportions, a beautiful Savior. He is encountered in the church: in the words of the liturgy, in the hymns, and, of course, in the Bible. Ecclesiastical traditions attest to the credibility of the reports concerning his life, death, and resurrection. Pictures, stained-glass windows, movies, Christmas crèches, outdoor billboards, signs on the back bumpers of automobiles ("Jesus Saves") and on banks ("Jesus Saves: So Can You"), traditional attitudes, the traditional reverential tone of voice, and stylized references to him in prayer have eventually made Jesus Christ into a wistful caricature, a— Christlike figure.

The average Protestant has manufactured a lovely Christ of outstanding past importance, an importance immeasurably greater than that of George Washington, Martin Luther, or Paul the apostle. However greater he may be thought to be, Jesus nonetheless, in the view of the average Protestant, is a past, *dead* figure who differs from other dead figures of international fame only in the fact that he proceeded to heaven in a more spectacular fashion. Mr. Protestant is decisively, categorically, and directly oriented to the past. He accepts the Golden Rule and the more general Sermon on the Mount, as well as the Ten Commandments, as morally normative, not because they are vivid teachings that appear strikingly out of his immediate future, concerning this deed to this neighbor, this act at this time, but because they have been attested to by wise and good men. In the past these teachings remain, along with the Magna Charta, the Declaration of Independence, and *The Diary of Anne Frank.* A distance of centuries dulls the voice of the teachings; their age imports to them a covering of psychological moss. They belong to the irretrievable "then" and are reverenced safely!

Mr. Protestant at "study" exercises more concern for conserving the traditions concerning Jesus Christ—and the traditional distance—than he does for the contents of the tradition or the meaning of the distance. Materials do in fact come to him out of his future. He reads a book, or an article in a curriculum piece, or the Bible. The reading of the words has never before happened, even if the words are the hallowed, memorized, profaned words "Do unto others . . ." The student, nonetheless, has read these words countless times; he knows them by heart, he reveres them and political leaders who revere them. They are not fresh words that teach him to do something immediate and graphic to others who have names and addresses. They are old words. They bear no message.

They are not Word of God. They reinforce his appreciation of an ecclesiastical tradition that teaches these old words qua old words to each new generation. In this sense the student is blocked to his future of grace. He cannot appropriate these tokens of God's favor which would raise him from death to life. He, in fact, redoubles his commitment to the past, to the world (with its judgment that doing unto others is a good thing that should be taught to the young in the public schools), and to his death-destined course of life.

The ecclesiastical mind-set, as described by Will Herberg, is pious and Biblicistic, tolerant of Buddhism and committed to a doctrine of inerrant verbal inspiration, other-centered and diffuse in social life and intensely personalistic in ecclesiastical life. The contradictions that describe and rule the mind of the average adult find their explanation in the fundamental allegiance of the adult to his past. The past is double-minded. Loyal to the past, the adult is consequently double-minded, but his allegiance is single-minded. One part of his revivalistic-frontier past leads him to affirm an inward, personal atonement substantiated by the verbally inspired, divine words in the Bible. Jesus Christ died for *him*. In some kind of heavenly transaction, which is seldom thought through by the adult—to whom the name Anselm would mean nothing at all—God took away his sins. All the adult must do is believe.

But another part of his past leads him to affirm the social consequences of his faith. This is one of the distinctive features of American Protestantism. Christianity must "make a difference." Moral living should issue from going to church. Better, happier life is promised to the churchgoer as he takes his "religion" home, to work, to school, etc. The neighborhood gathering at the outdoor barbecue is a response to the past, even though the elders of another day would be scandalized by the martinis. The group Bible study reformulates without essentially changing the mandate of the past, expressed for another time in the idyllic Robert Burns portrait of *The Cotter's Saturday Night*.

With both sides of the tradition set in unseemly nearness,

their obvious contradictions are exaggerated, but they are exaggerated in such a way that their traditional appeal is emphasized. Fundamentalism and togetherness, so often found desirable by the same person, represent a yet deeper commitment to the substantial goodness of the yesteryear. Cut a man off from tradition as Wright Morris does in his brilliant novel, *The Works of Love*, and he eventually jumps into the river. Shear a man from loyalty to the past, leaving him with ambiguous feelings of sympathy and antagonism toward it and you have *Miss Lonelyhearts*, that grotesquely perceptive creation of Nathaniel West. Leave a man in untouched communion with his past and you have the mildly troubled, vaguely hostile adult encountered in adult study.

This student is more American than Protestant, more American Protestant than Christian. Troubled he may be, but he has by no means given up on the past to which he has pledged his devotion. Doré Schary, an accomplished and articulate movie director, believes that we are going to find reflections of the American character in the movies that are most successful, i.e., that draw the most Americans. This is a statistically doubtful proposition, because the most Americans who see a particular movie do not represent the American character. Many Americans, for instance, have ceased going to movies. But theologically, Mr. Schary is on safer grounds. The American character is reflected in the mirror of the movies that precisely the most Americans find attractive. At any rate, the following is what Schary finds.

I don't think it is any accident that the most durable and best patronized type of movie is the Western. Westerns continue to be made for the simple reason that customers flock to see them, and producers know they have a steady market for them. One Western may vary infinitesimally from another; it doesn't seem to matter. I think it is because the Western stirs in all of us pride and admiration of our own heritage—a heritage we owe to the men of a new nation who carved its history with tomahawk and knife and secured it with shotgun and raw endurance. The details of an individual Western are secondary: what is irresistible, apparently, is that the old, beloved tale of a good man winning over insurmountable odds, defeating the bad man in an honorable way, is being retold. In a way, we are repeatedly honoring the heroes who were our forebears; it is a kind of ritual offering to their memory.

As Americans, we love a hero, a winner, a champion. It is not in the American character to be drawn to a loser, no matter how honorably he lost. This may not be good, but it is true all the same. We are impatient of anything short of success.[17]

And yet, "Americans also have a strange but sneaking admiration for con men and resourceful hucksters who live by their wits, getting something for nothing and operating (correctly) on the Barnum theory that there's one born every minute. The admiration goes back, I think, to our esteem for the loner, the man on his own who makes up his own rules, plays the long shots, and sees them pay off. Even the victim can only gasp in admiring outrage at how he has been taken. He chalks it up to experience and does little else, because by now the hoaxer is well on his way out of town. The victim concedes, ruefully and with a kind of respect, that he has been outsmarted. Americans do go by this curious rule, and it is another facet of our highly competitive natures. The hustler has always been a folk character, colorful, breezy, friendly, and larcenous, and we are usually pleased to see him get away with it. We are pleased and amused to read that the Brooklyn Bridge is still changing ownership regularly, that iceboxes are being sold to Eskimos, and that there's still a brisk business in the gold-brick trade. The great W. C. Fields became a major star by portraying this typically American character in a number of memorable film variations on the same theme. We immediately warm to the character because he's a go-getter, enterprising and indomitable. And it's fun to be fooled. Let him not get caught, though. Once that happens, he's no smarter than the rest of us and we have no use for him, and no more affection. Because he's a cheat and a liar? No; because he isn't very good at it.[18]

[17] Doré Schary, "Our Movie Mythology," *The Reporter* (March 3, 1960), p. 39.
[18] *Ibid.*, p. 41.

The general respect for the heroic winner *and* the creative hustler that Schary finds in the American character has more bearing on the conduct of the Christian education of adults than educators are prepared to admit. Before figures in the liturgical and traditional past can be found acceptable by the typical Protestant, they must undergo subtle transformations, must be remade, idealized. This remaking does, of course, happen regularly in adult study, and not only to Jesus Christ, whose fate in America seems to lie in being cast in a role at once Lincolnian and Lone Rangerish. The apostles are idealized; David becomes a super Eagle Scout sort of person—continuing a process that the editors of II Samuel to I Kings began. Books on great men and women in the Bible (note specifically the sentimental biographies of Old Testament ladies and gentlemen found in Fleming James's *Personalities of the Old Testament*) transform normative Hebrew types into classical American types. This is true not only of Ruth but of Miriam, not only of Abraham but of Jacob-Israel—probably the most un-American character in Biblical literature.

The attempt to arrange all history into American categories, of course, is intellectually and psychologically dishonest, but that consideration does not apparently inhibit the attempt. American Protestants are committed to the past, and until that commitment is repented of, educators should learn to expect that adult learners will make decisions that are consonant with their basic commitment. They repudiate insights into their future. Their Americanizing of history includes hoping—wistfully no doubt, but nonetheless hoping—that the future will merely "work out all right." Thus they are aligned by the very course of their life against the good news concerning God's majestic and gracious future activity. Typically, they are busy with the pedestrian endeavor entitled, of all things, "Relating the Gospel to Everyday Life." Making the past words say something about present life reveals the sinister malaise: the adult students do not look with eyes of faith toward what is coming. As such they are willfully ignorant of the good news, malignantly, antagonistically ignorant of the Bible. They are blocked, and this living fact is what makes *Christian* education impossible.

The valence assigned to Biblical ignorance makes an immense difference for determining procedures of Christian education. I have been defining Biblical ignorance as a willful refusal to deal with the good news concerning what God is about to do. This definition emphasizes, laterally, the commitment of the will to the ideas and proved experience of the past. Many educators believe that Biblical ignorance should be located in the mind instead of the will. This belief drives them to define the job of Christian education as providing Biblical knowledge to the illiterate. The illiterate in this context are thought of as people who do not know, but who can be helped to learn, the Bible.

In an article appearing in *The Christian Century* a pastor tells us that he suspected that the members of his congregation had only the foggiest ideas about elementary Biblical matters. He thus sprang a quiz on the congregation. The questions he prepared "were of a kind that any older Sunday school pupil or anyone with a general knowledge of the Bible could be expected to answer correctly. Most of them took the form of easy terms that could be identified in a word or at most a simple sentence. A 90 per cent score ought to have been universal." But the congregation did not score as it should have, according to the pastor's expectations. I shall quote the revealing final paragraphs of the article.

There was complete confusion as to the number of converts baptized by Jesus, ranging from none (correct) to 300,000. Jesus was variously listed as living under Julius Caesar, King Saul, and King Solomon. More serious is the congregation's lack of knowledge as to the two great commandments. Answers to this question ranged over the whole realm of ethics, with the Seventh Commandment getting several votes. One person, who apparently objected to the test, wrote on his paper, "Is religion history?"

Obviously he was unaware that the Christian faith is historically grounded and that we do not truly know that faith unless we know the situations in which men discovered God's word.

Here are the test questions and the grading of the answers (one of the questions was used in both tests):

QUESTION	% WITH CORRECT OR SEMICORRECT ANSWERS
Calvary	77
The Exodus	66
Thomas	60
The Gospels	58
Nazareth	58
Gethsemane	57
Elijah	56
The Two Great Commandments	55
Ruler under whom Jesus lived	43
Samaritans	39
Zacchaeus	35
Bartholomew	28
The Sower	26
Pentecost	23
The Macedonian Call	22
The New Jerusalem	20
Amos (the man)	19
The Exile	18
Number baptized by Jesus	17

Over-all tabulation of the returns gave the following results:

SCORE		% WITH THIS SCORE
0–45	Biblically illiterate	63
50–65	Sketchy knowledge	20
70–85	Good	12
90–100	Excellent	5

In evaluating the results, it must be borne in mind that while most of the 300 adults who took the test were members of the congregation, a substantial number were nonmember visitors. Even so, it seems plain that Biblical ignorance is the rule among members of one particular congregation. If other Protestant con-

gregations are like ours, Christian education still has a long way
to go.[19]

No one will argue with Rev. Mr. Pendell's conclusion, but
a great deal of thought should be given to the direction that
Christian education takes in the "long way" it still has to go.
What actually did the quiz demonstrate that might be helpful
in charting the long way? Might Christian educators assume
that a course on elementary facts of the Bible would solve the
problem? Is Bible lore, furnished in attractive, up-to-date educational packages, going to solve illiteracy, to say nothing of
ignorance? To be blunt, will knowledge of the exact content
of the great comandment remove a student from the ranks of
the illiterate or the ignorant? And, conversely, does the fact
that a person has not scored well on that question mean that
he does not love God, then his neighbor as himself?

Although some doubts are making their disagreeable presence felt in the councils of denominational specialists, the
present position of adult education in the church is firmly in
line with the assumptions of *The Christian Century* article.
People are not in possession of elementary Biblical facts. Hence
they are illiterate. But they can be educated by making the
facts available in the context of advanced educational methods.
The amazing fact is that no irate educator or theologian wrote
a letter to the editor of the magazine (a generally approved
indoor sport among many American Protestants) protesting the
use of a quiz in lieu of a sermon explicating a Biblical text.
The quiz was itself a technique used to provide the pastor with
dependable information and, no doubt, to dramatize to the
congregation its need for Biblical education.

The people who answered the quiz have not responded well
to the ordinary, standard educational opportunities afforded
them. Either they have not learned or have not availed themselves of learning opportunities. The sermons have proved ineffective. Therefore, argue the specialists, the standard situa-

[19] Thomas R. Pendell, "Biblical Literacy Test," *The Christian Century*
(October 21, 1959), p. 1213.

tions must be reshaped. The students should be introduced to new kinds of study experience in which they can, for one thing, expose their ignorance instead of hiding behind a veil of silence. They should have opportunity to talk out misconceptions and to "try new ideas on for size." Above all, the students should be helped to relax and be as ignorant as they really are. Admission of the real situation is a kind of indispensable beginning for a project of real learning.

The specialists of almost every denomination (including those of some traditionally conservative groups) are unanimous in suggesting that the Bible be met on its own terms, in its own idiom, by people who are prepared to find out what it has to say. But what it has to say turns out to be "what it says to you." Through frank discussion the learner is helped to see that his thoughts about the Bible are as important as those of the next person. The learner becomes reader and thinker. He encounters the Bible as it is and discusses what he has found with other readers and thinkers in open exchange of ideas and opinions. The learner is thus taught that he must be responsible for what he learns. He cannot depend on a lecturer or a professional source of information to give him the results of their thinking. He must think things through for himself.

Because most existing educational situations are not flexible enough to provide this sort of Bible study, the denominational specialists rightly plead for new groupings, at meeting times preferably during the week instead of on Sunday mornings at the traditional time. The specialists have seen that custom precludes very much constructive change in the rigidly stylized formal Sunday morning adult Bible class. They suggest the establishment of week-night groups in order to make possible new experiences with Bible study.

But rarely in the suggestions offered by a denomination to a church full of Biblical illiterates is a clarifying remark made about the illiteracy itself. The tacit assumption seems to be that all the interested people who enroll in a Bible-study course or consent to participate in a study group will learn the Bible as a matter of course. As far as the specialists are concerned, the problem is poor teaching method currently being employed and poor teaching situations. Change these, they infer, and learning will take place. The specialists should be commended for their almost athletic attempts to break up the stodgy, inept, hopelessly tradition-bound adult Sunday school class. They have rightly seen that the stereotyped ideas that the learners hold toward Bible study inhibits real study. But they have slight chances of winning their battle with illiteracy until they come to see that illiteracy is a thin masquerade for ignorance and that ignorance is not overcome by knowledge, even when masterfully taught.

Sara Little's *Learning Together in the Christian Fellowship,* as good a book as there is in the field, presents an almost idyllic picture of the ways in which effective method and sound procedure can team up against ignorance. This idyll presumes: (*a*) a Christian fellowship, (*b*) the best educational procedures, and (*c*) eagerness among the learners to learn something. Surely the evidence of life in the ordinary Protestant church with its typical American Protestants makes the idyll not only out of place but almost sad. Having done all that she so expertly suggests, the leader of a study group might hope that the sessions will be more interesting, worth working at, talking about, and studying for. But he has no reason to hope that the group will become Biblically faithful.

The opposite of ignorance, when we come right down to the realities, is not knowledge, but faith. Churchly education can, under optimum circumstances, supply knowledge to churchmen. Education in general has the means for helping people to be able to pass a literacy quiz that a pastor might spring any Sunday. But neither churchly education nor general education can hope to touch the deep, corelike resistance of the learner to the message that the Bible presents. And distinctively Christian education, i.e., education that takes the adjective "Christian" seriously, assumes that Christians are speaking to one another about the new things that God is doing among them, even as they open themselves to the record of God's activities in other times with his people. In faith alone is ignorance robbed of its power, and the creation of faith belongs exclusively within the province of God's Spirit.

Adult education does not have access to the historical situation in which learning is planned to take place. Adult education cannot hope to change the church or the community, rewrite the past, or overcome the stubbornness with which "students" persist in accepting the Jesus Christ of the past in the Bible of the past from the church interested in solidifying its traditional claims on them. Exactly this situation accounts for the puzzling lack of results that characterizes the best, most widely touted situations. By determined effort, students maintain a last-ditch stand against the Bible. Thus adult education, in assuming that illiteracy and ignorance are the same thing, in planning programs that allow the learner to distort the Biblical message through free informal discussion, i.e., Americanization of Biblical materials, has, if anything, deepened the ignorance. The typical student, as a typical human being, according to the Bible, is antigospel, anti-Jesus Christ, anti-God; pro-past, pro-world, pro-lies, and pro-death.

There is a sense in which the Bible should not be thought of as study material; surely it should not be used as a sophisticated gimmick in order to enlist the support of a lot of tradition-bound folks in a successful study program; surely it should not be trotted out in answer to the traditional yearnings of the people for a god and his word. Yet it is. This kind of performance led Sören Kierkegaard over a hundred years ago to suggest that all the Bibles in the land be taken up on a hill and burned. That, in our day, would produce a big fire, and in the long run might be most effective in making the cure for Biblical ignorance possible.

My aim is to teach you to pass from a piece of disguised nonsense to something that is patent nonsense.[20]—*L. Wittgenstein.*

[20] L. Wittgenstein, *Philosophical Investigations*, tr. by G. E. M. Anscombe (B. H. Blackwell, Ltd., Oxford, 1953), p. 133.

Chapter 5

VENTURING IN FAITH

While I was editing a denominational adult curriculum magazine, 90 per cent of the correspondence I received complained of the intellectual difficulty of the curriculum materials. A startling number of these letters were composed according to the stereotyped formula inherited from an anti-intellectual past. The writers supposed that curriculum should be simple, down to earth, helpful in personal matters, and crowded with Bible reference. Many pastors wrote such letters in behalf of their irate laymen, concurring with the lay opinion. Set in the context of the Christian education of adults as we have been dealing with it in the first part of this book, such a reaction is not surprising at all. Strictly intellectual concerns have received short notice from educators, and the churches have traditionally been apathetic to such concerns. Educational time has been spent on devotion, the spiritual life, affection, warmth, personality growth, emotional unfolding, nonverbal communication, and analysis of personal relations, but precious little time has been spent on ideas. Customized, stripped-down ideas, when they have been introduced educationally into an educational situation, have worn the habit of a gimmick, designed, that is, to stimulate discussion, meeting, and growth, but not necessarily intellectual activity.

The remainder of this book is going to be concerned with intellectual activity, with forming the church as a small university, with looking at the group as a library and clearing-house for ideas, with thinking pastors in thinking churches, with the birth of mental passion, with the growth of conceptual ability, with the nurture of tough minds. The church has other functions to perform. People die, sue for divorce, become psychotic. The church has a ministry to them, but it is not an educational ministry. People who have never been confronted with the gospel need to hear the gospel. But evangelism is not an educational matter. People are worried, estranged, in need of support and encouragement. They should get their help, but not directly from educators. People need to pray and to learn how to pray, but an educator can only teach them to think about prayer. We shall be considering education's primary job and how to get it done and in the act we shall be trimming down the omnibus goals that Christian education has accrued to one goal: teaching. Children's educators say to one another, "Don't treat children as though they were little adults." Adult educators have not said but should say to one another, "Don't treat adults as though they were big children."

An Acknowledgment

Mr. Paul Goodman has had the last word—so far—on John Dewey and the progressive education that that great American envisioned. Goodman calls progressive education one, among many, of our unfinished revolutions.[21] It has been aborted by technocrats. Dewey taught teachers to set up a play store in order to build up some desire in little children to learn arithmetic. The teachers heard "store," set up the store, and allowed the children to play "store" until they were tired. This analysis is of course unfair, specifically to the good teachers who have done good jobs in teaching arithmetic. But Goodman's thesis is generally fair, and it is scalding. Stopping with

[21] Paul Goodman, *Growing Up Absurd* (Random House, Inc., 1960).

Dewey's famous five steps, in problem-solving dramatically curtails a revolution because the revolution imagined by Dewey was going to supply the problem solvers with ingenuity and ideas that could be thrown into the business of solving problems. Dewey's whole educational program presupposes a mentally well-equipped Democrat, an heir of the American legacy, a salty pragmatist whose belief in pragmatic method is at once passionate and for that reason unpragmatic. The problem solver has got to want his community to be a wonderful community, or else the democratic energies that stand behind education, ennoble and fructify it, become corrosive and manipulative. Mr. Goodman makes that point clear. Americans have given up their passionately unpragmatic belief in pragmatism and have become, therefore, tinhorn hucksters—in education as well as at the market place.

I don't propose now to have the church finish John Dewey's revolution, although that would be considerably more important than most of the jobs it is presently busy with. I have drawn attention to this matter of problem solving because I want to draw attention to what lies behind problem solving: the mentally equipped, spiritually alert, interested, and curious man who has passionate convictions about the worth of his community and about working with his fellow community members in order to get at what ails his community. Dewey, of course, has been a convenient whipping boy for ill-assorted educational and theological reactionaries. But, ironically, he shows the way to Protestant educators. They should have the wit to see that his avowed nontheism does not endanger the Christian faith but indirectly affirms it. His fame lies in espousing pragmatic methodology; his greatness can be found in his vision. And it is Dewey the visionary who should command Protestant educators to look where he looked. I would be unfair not to acknowledge that Dewey's vision has fascinated me, while a host of thundering theists has pointed the way backward to nonvisions, to yesterday, to the boredom and ineffectuality of the same old thing.

Charismatic Events

So much attention can be given to how a man thinks that what he thinks about slides away in unimportance. What comes into his mind? What occupies him? What absorbs him? And consider another range of questions that consequently become important. In what manner does he deal with the stuff that has entered his mind? To what does he relate the stuff? Into what region does he reach for a device with which to size it up? And—what is the outcome? That, too, must be asked.

The classical way in which classical epistemological questions are dealt with by classical epistemologists—from Aristotle to Ayer—obscures the weight of the questions themselves for the nonclassical man who happens to be thinking about nonclassical matters such as the electric bill. And the life of the mind is taken up mostly with nonclassical stuff that is partially a blend of memories and anticipations and partially a running interior flow of words made in commentary on the life that is going on outside the thinker. Ideas come at a man, epistemologically considered, in exactly the same manner that a tree or a baseball or a child comes at him. But the peculiar difference in what enters his mind! It matters very little to the tree whether or not it is seen in its splendid wholeness, momentarily a creature before another creature. But it matters a great deal to the man that he is ready to deal with trees as creatures. And if trees, so too ideas, and even more so, children.

The options available to man as he thinks vary according to whatever it is that has just come at him. A man is reading the newspaper. The words come at him. His political and social orientation predispose him to look at "the news" as though it were a re-enactment of the same old stuff he has always been reading in newspapers. This may be a wise choice. The words flow across him, as it were, without engaging him. In the very act of reading the newspaper he has chosen *not* to be bothered.

He wants to get to the sports page anyway, or to the funnies.
And what does he choose to do with *these* words and pictures?
He has unfinished stories, now, things that he has no knowledge about. "You can depend on politicians' being crooks,"
he says, "but you do not know for sure who is going to win
the National League pennant, or how Dr. Morgan is going to
handle his latest patient and whether or not he will marry his
pretty nurse." Our man chooses to be interested in these
affairs, although they are inconsequential compared to the
import of the words on the front page reporting a budget hike
or a new, successful test firing of an atomic device.

Likewise a child comes at the man: "it" can suddenly become to him a visitation by a child—his child—; "it" can
represent an invasion of his relaxation and privacy; "it" can be
the source of a lot of words to which he must dutifully respond.
Knowing that the child can be any one of these different
children, the man chooses to drop the newspaper to be ready
for whatever happens: a visitation, an invasion, or an uninteresting chat. He might, of course, have protected himself
from any of these happenings by closing the door beforehand;
and he might, on the other hand, have anticipated which
child was coming in on him and dealt with *that* child no matter
which child has in fact determined to come at him.

It is a great mistake to presume that thinking is a regular
process describable prior to what is being thought about. The
things that come at a man differ widely, and they can be
thought about in such an astonishing variety of ways. One
substantial, if not general, point, can, however, be made. In
thinking, a man fundamentally either disposes himself willingly toward the new stuff that is constantly coming at him
or he is indifferent to it or he sees it in such a way that it can
be ignored. Karen Horney has explored the psychiatric dimensions of these modes or dispositions toward the continual
occurrence of the new. Her insights have special bearing in
the area of what happens to make a man give up one disposition in favor of another. Also, Rudolf Bultmann has
explored these dispositions in Pauline *and* Heideggerian terms,

calling one disposition an openness to or readiness for the command of *God*, the indifferent mode a stoic mind-set, and the ignoring mode an expression of having a blocked future and enslavement to the world (which is described thus as the place where the past continues to re-enact itself).

The crucial matter for thought turns out to be the pre-dispositions of the man who is encountering such and such stuff. Predispositions are prior to thought, and thinking about *them*, that is, representing them before the mind as stuff to think about, does not thereby alter their power or cause them to go away. A man who has blocked himself to his future cannot openly consider his blockedness, because he *is* blocked and fights against the new idea that is presented to him. He has no ability to deal with this idea. It may attract him, momentarily fill him with wonder about himself, force him open just long enough for him to see its power. But he discards it; in his scorn toward it he *exhibits* its truth and power. Conversely, the man who fundamentally is willing to be open to whatever comes along deals with the idea that he is blocked. He freely considers this idea. It concerns him. It fills him with uneasiness. He fights the possibility of its truth, to be sure, but his openness leads him to examine how it is that he may have blocked himself from the new. In his openness he is led to remorse for his stubbornness. He openly turns toward the new once more to find what it has in store for him.

Let us here consider the fighting that goes on no matter what predisposition governs a man's thought. Man has contentedly attached himself to *his* way of thinking. It is, after all, *his*. He may think of himself as a poor and humble thinker, a Pooh Bear who contents himself with the knowledge that he is a bear of little brain. But he is content with just *this* thinking about himself. Comes an intruder. The most open man in the world gathers himself up at the appearance of a potential challenger. The most friendly man in the world asks "friend or foe?" when *his* friendliness is attacked. God can afford to smile at blasphemers, but man cannot. Man does not want to be questioned. He prefers living on peacefully in his way, even if that way happens to be a way of perennial con-

flict. He seems constitutionally indisposed to deal easily with
stuff that harries him to analysis. As a consequence, he fights.
The intruder is berated, ignored, called names; then, according to predisposition, the intruder is told to sit down or is cast
out. But never without a fight.

An omnivorous intellectual has troubles with new ideas to
quite the same extent as the nonreader. The intellectual is
merely more acute. He reads things that fit him and suit his
ideas, while the nonreader as contentedly stays within the
safe confines of his predictable little universe, worries a bit
over a flashing thought but manages to keep the universe
intact (and I could be talking about a psychotic universe as
well as a *Reader's Digest* universe). For this reason the *Book
Review* section of *The New York Times* almost always can be
counted on to be as safe as *The Reader's Digest*. The *Book
Review* is comfortably predictable. Nothing so outrageous as
an idea that contravenes the prevailing style appears there.
The Squares treat the Beats badly, and the Beats treat the
Squares badly. The reviews of important fiction deal with
successful fiction importantly because this is the way things
now stand for the intellectual readers who make *The New
York Times Book Review* a Sunday afternoon fixture. Which
points up a truism held sacred by the entire human race:
dodge a fight if you can, but if you prefer fighting, dodge any
fight with the idea that you should give up fighting.

The potentially challenging nature of the stuff that provokes
thinking can, to an extent, account for the inevitable pain and
duress that accompanies thought and makes it an often dreadful proceeding. Giving assent to reassuring stuff, and ignoring
the rest, actually is a fiction. No stuff is that reassuring, and
no assent has that tea party easiness. The quick assent, "Yes,
this is what I agree with," merely hides the flashing recognition, takes no note of the *aperçu*. Even here the potentially
challenging, the potentially painful lie in wait around a
corner which therefore is not turned. And in the stuff that
cannot be equally accepted, the challenge and the threat of
pain are, of course, immediately present. The man in thought
has gotten himself into trouble. He has allowed himself to be

forced to reconsider, to reflect. He must re-examine and walk reluctantly down an old path to its source in order to see, as suggested by the stuff, whether a new path is not better. New information throws his old information into suspicion. New possibilities force him to contemplate them and to give up possibilities that he has already decided on. A new idea startles him and more often than not makes him afraid, because his very own, dearly loved, ideas are placed under a cloud of doubt. Who wants confusion? Who *likes* to be tormented? No one. Because no one remains essentially ready to deal with painful uncertainty—and that readiness is the sure sign of the free, *thinking* man.

Whenever a man thinks, and no matter about what, that man is exerting himself toward what is going on. He bestirs himself and absorbs himself with what is going on. The activity is mental, but it is nonetheless activity as remarkable as that of a lazy, fat old man deliberately going out for a ten-mile hike. And this activity, at once painful and remarkable, whether issuing in acceptance, rejection, or ignoring of the stuff, is properly the life of the mind. With such activity education is superlatively concerned.

Rudolf Bultmann's essay *The Historicity of Man and Faith*, which deals with the relationship of philosophy with theology, has a great deal to say about the relationship that we are now obliged to consider, namely, the relationship of education to Christian education, the relationship of general epistemology to Christian thought. Bultmann in what is to me his most challenging single essay declares against his critic Gerhardt Kuhlmann that "the object of an existential analysis of man is man; and it is likewise man that is the object of theology . . . the theme of philosophy (at any rate, so far as man falls within its realm) is *the natural man*, while the theme of theology is *the man of faith*."[22]

[22] Rudolf Bultmann, *Existence and Faith: The Shorter Writings of Rudolf Bultmann* (Meridian Books, Inc., 1960), p. 93.

This is the passage I wish to quote:

> Theologically expressed, faith is not a new quality that in-
> heres in the believer, but rather a possibility of man that must
> constantly be laid hold of anew because man only exists by con-
> stantly laying hold of his possibilities. That man of faith does not
> become an angel, but is *simul peccator, simul iustus.* Therefore,
> all of the basic Christian concepts have a content that can be
> determined ontologically prior to faith and in a purely rational
> way. All theological concepts contain the understanding of being
> that belongs to man as such and by himself in so far as he exists
> at all. Thus theology should indeed learn from philosophy—
> precisely from that philosophy "which confesses as its deepest
> determination to 'serve the work of Dilthey,' which is to say,
> man's understanding of himself qua man."[23]

We have now explicated some flavor of thought and have
gone so far as to call readiness "to deal with painful uncertainty— . . . the sure sign of the free, *thinking* man." Is the
plain man as capable of such thinking? Is he "free," therefore,
in the same way that the Christian is? To turn the question
another way: Does the Christian achieve his education as any
man does? Is the content of general education and Christian
education the same? In answer to these questions Bultmann's
idea sounds a challenge that we must consider, whether or
not it is distasteful. His idea leads us to perceive no difference
in thinking, no matter who is thinking. Pagan American man
thinks. So does Christian man. So does Hindu man. Likewise,
Bultmann prompts us to construct no false distinctions between general education and Christian education. In both
cases the object of education is the same: thinking man. But
this is by no means the end of the matter. Bultmann uses the
word "faith" to mean "a possibility of man that must constantly be laid hold of anew because man only exists by
constantly laying hold of his possibilities." And *the* possibility
of man that can be called faith is not *any* possibility. It is not
laid hold of by every man. Here is a specified possibility:

That revelation has actually encountered [the man of faith],

23 *Ibid.,* p. 96.

that he really lives, that he is in fact graced, that he is really forgiven and will always be so. And he knows this in such a way that by faith in the revelation his concrete life in work and in joy, in struggle and in pain is newly qualified; he knows that through the *event* of revelation the events of his life become new —"new" in the sense that is valid only for the man of faith and visible only to him, that indeed only *becomes* visible in the now and thus must always become visible *anew*. The only new thing that faith and faith alone is able to say about revelation is that it has become an event and becomes an event.[24]

Faith as a possibility that is laid hold of now does seem to qualify the kind of thinking that might be thought of as characteristically Christian. Temptations surely do exist, particularly in American Protestantism so victimized by effeminate pietism, to describe Christian thinking in terms not of its quality but of its sacred contents. The Christian, in contradistinction to the pagan, thinks about Jesus Christ and the Bible, about goodness and the church, about sin and faith. Faith thus becomes meditation upon itself. Yet, do not other people also think about sacred contents? Philosophers of religion, sociologists, newspaper reporters, Buddhist scholars, and Communist cell organizers—people not generally well thought of by American Christians as Christian types—think about sacred subjects. And are *they* therefore Christian? Faith meditating upon itself and its own sacred contents, and defining the meditation as faith, is amusing and foolish. It is because of such temptations that any expression like "Christian thinking" or "faithful thinking" automatically appears dubious. Yet not even pietism can frighten away what seems clearly to be the situation. The man of faith thinks not about different things but about the same things as any other man— but from a peculiar perspective, in a different way, and occasionally with a different outcome. So we do, after all, have a Christian thinking that is specifically and uniquely Christian because it is faithful. And we do, then, have a Christian education that proceeds not along unique courses, but that sees

24 *Ibid.*, p. 100.

thinking as a peculiar charismatic event, in just such a way
that general education would find either unbelievable or—
unthinkable. We do, that is, if we can accept Rudolf Bultmann's analysis of the relationship of natural man to the man
of faith, and, of greater importance, if we can live with his
analysis of the "faith" part of his expression "man of faith."

This is no place to enter into a full-length discussion of
Bultmann's general method and position—that would require
a book much bigger than this one. And his general method and
position actually have very little to do with the problem of the
usefulness of his instruction to the issue at hand, namely,
Christian thinking vis-à-vis ordinary, mortal, human thinking.
The problem occurs at the point of defining faith as he does in
terms of a possibility for man rather than in terms of the divine
gift to man. This was what worried Gerhardt Kuhlmann. He
was afraid that Bultmann had given up his stance as an
evangel by making use of the Heideggerian analysis of existence and being and by using some Heideggerian language
in order to explicate the good news. But what is there to be
afraid of here? Why should the Christian flinch over the very
thought that he differs from no man? His re-creation, as Paul
calls it, is at best a daily resurrection from the dead and not
some spectacular ontological development that can be duly
charted by Christian theologians. Is his faith not this: that his
life is graced, that he sees it as graced, that he beholds on the
frontier of his life the graciousness of God, that he, indeed,
has a future of grace? Is not faith, then, a kind of stubbornness, a predisposition to look into the future with eyes of
faith, so that the looking becomes an accepting of the tokens
of God's favor? Not a once-for-all divine gift, faith is willingness to accept a graced life that perceives the *continued* flow
of divine gifts. And how else could it be? The revelation has
become an event in Jesus Christ, and that is precisely *the* event
by which entry is made, not into a newness of life that is
ontologically new, but into a newness of life that is ontologically identical to natural life yet that is acceptable as constantly and radically new.

Thinking is a charismatic event for the man of faith. So too is mowing the lawn and talking to a neighbor. Yet thinking is the charismatic event par excellence because it comprehends the activities of mowing the lawn or reading the newspaper or talking to a neighbor or welcoming a child. It is happening in just such a way that these casual, recurring items of every-day life can be understood as the occasions that God graciously provides. Matthew, ch. 25, drives us to look at these daily habitual rounded-off certainties in a peculiar eschatological, yea, a Christological, light. But they become enlightened in thought. They are found to be new events by a willingness and a freedom to welcome, and if not welcome, at least accept, the contents of casual life as eschatological tokens.

Christian education teaches what the thinking man does not have within him. If he does not know the history of Roman civilization, he is taught to know the Romans and, with a peculiar sensitivity, to know how the Romans made up their laws, how they lived together, what their life together amounted to, what it produced, who its lawyers and priests and emperors were, how long their civilization lasted, what led to its beginning, and what caused it to crumble. Christian education cannot teach the man how to gain the peculiar sensitivity. It can, of course, teach him to think about the peculiar sensitivity as an idea. That is all. The thinking man has it or is granted it as a predisposition. Reading about Roman civilization can be for him a charismatic event that proceeds from his own future as a brand-new occurrence. To the extent that he becomes bigger inside, Christian education has worked.

Christian education deals with thinking, but from the perspective that thinking is a charismatic event. That is its only distinction and its true glory. Like all education, it is concerned with the enlargement of thinking. Along with education in general it aims at making a man bigger on the inside. It provides him with information and gives him a truth-filled past. Education points out to him the issues of the day and forces in on him with a constant pressure to organize and discipline his thought. Honesty and humility before the phenomena are thus not to be conceived primarily as a distinctive attribute of the scientist, who can be unscrupulous when dealing with phenomena that do not fit his definition of phenomena or his canons of meaning. Honesty and humility are the achievements of any educated man before any stuff that comes at him.

Christian education proceeds toward the enlargement of thinking. It finds, with all education, that its chief allies are plain ordinary curiosity and extraordinary imagination. Its foes, too, are the same, to wit: reaction, prejudice, disinterest, and fanaticism. Christian education seeks not to give or to help or to save or to convert, but to teach the thinking man to think.

Fred Denbeaux claims that Protestants are related to the past fundamentally through books. He calls the Protestant Church a community of scholars. He also uses an expression that has an appealing evangelical ring. He refers to the "thrill of learning." These things are found in his book entitled *Understanding the Bible*.[25] Because he talks primarily about the Bible, his remarks concerning the honesty it compels and the sweat necessary to come to grips with it seem to be centered exclusively on the Bible, as more or less nontransferable items. Yet, for the reason that Protestants do have that one book, they own a special fondness and an enduring zeal for books—any books. Denbeaux might not have written the same things as he did about understanding the Bible if he had been writing on understanding William Faulkner or Heraclitus—not to say that Faulkner and Heraclitus would have interested Protestant Americans—but he probably would have written much the same thing. Certainly he would have used "the thrill of learning," simply because it is an ingenious expression. Certainly he would have reminded the Protestant community

[25] Fred J. Denbeaux, *Understanding the Bible* (The Westminster Press, 1958).

of its functional definition as a community of scholars. The Bible drives Protestants away from itself into the world of books that are a part of the world as such. And because they have to be driven they go back to the Bible and learn once more that they should go from it. This is the grace of the Bible: that it refuses a reader's worship by pointing to his neighbor, to his book, to his grave, to his political rostrum, with the divine command: "Go!"

More on the subject of Bible study will soon be said. This much, however, cannot be postponed. The Bible itself drives Christian education out of Bible study. The Bible itself, by its own message *as* the Word of God, foments thinking about the frontier on which contemporary life comes into being. How can Christian education, then, if it has studied and thought with that peculiar graced sensitivity of faith, remain at Bible study, or worse yet, perform pious studies that are merely propaedeutics to Bible study?

Consider the Bible quiz recorded in Chapter Four. Most Christian educators bemoan the Biblical illiteracy that the statistics proved. True, the congregation performed poorly, and Christian educators should be alarmed. Now, had the pastor given an equally simple quiz on current events, what would he have discovered? And had he been even more evangelically curious, he might have sought some statistics on what the congregation had been reading, and without the aid of multiple-choice questions could have obtained some evidences of the quality of his congregation's thought. On these evidences the pastor might have discovered more surely the task that Christian education had yet to perform in his church. Our American tradition is so Biblicistic that Christian education turns automatically to the Bible because, for one thing, the people in the churches are Biblicistic and would not comprehend any other kind of study that Christian education proposed. In a Biblicistic tradition God has become boxed into the Bible. His grace proceeds through the Bible. So the God whom Karl Barth, on an epigrammatic tear, says can speak through any event or thing that he chooses—even a dead dog

—has in American churches allowed one manner of speech: King James English; one book to speak from: the Bible; and one people to speak to: Bible-believing Americans. What should Christian education do in such a situation? Laugh or weep?

Probably it should laugh *and* weep, preferably at the same time. But as it proceeds into action, it must, by demonstrative parabolic activity, contest the lie that Biblicism conceals. And this contest must be fought, in the best Kierkegaardian style, indirectly. Great ferocious words against Biblicism do not get close to the Biblicist. He casts them away with disdain. Intense Bible study would more likely reinforce his blocked thinking about the Bible than force him into open thinking. Looking up *charis* in a theological wordbook does not, even in Greek, open a man to grace. But, now, according to artful means proposed by Kierkegaard, such a book as *Prisoner of Grace*, by Joyce Cary, might be pushed toward the Biblicist as some stuff for thinking or perhaps as a potentially charismatic event. (Giving the book to him would surely be a charismatic event.) So the man begins his reading and reads the book straight through, identifying first with Jim, then Nina, and maybe for a second or so with the redoubtable Chester. What a complicated triangle this turns out to be! How could Mr. Cary possibly presume to use the word "grace" in connection with this book which features a doubly adulterous woman? Exactly. How could he? And which one of the three persons is the prisoner of grace? Exactly. Which one? What has God to do with people of this ilk? "And— *what have they to do with me?*" With that question the possibility has now been actualized. His future has burst open. There he stands before his future. Considerations of doctrinal purity retreat. The man has been laid hold of. Indirectly, of course, his Biblicism has been dealt a mortal blow, which was the goal of the contest. But that counts very little. Of immeasurably greater importance is his inside, which is now bigger by one book. He will now come to any new book or any new experience or to the Bible with this book as a part of his expanded thinking. He will have known the thrill of learning.

A *Thinking Church*

A church begins to think when it is forced to think by seeing, in its midst, a thinking man who is interested in what they think and how they think. Rigorous attention to Protestant polity makes us single out the pastor as the chief thinker of the church. He already is the chief teacher, at least according to his ordination. It would be nice if the chief teacher were the chief thinker. Whether likely or not, it must nonetheless be assumed. No one else in a church has the churchly prestige that the pastor has, and consequently no one else's demonstrative activity would precipitate such violent consternation, i.e., thought. Conceivably, a thinking church could be made to think by someone other than its pastor. But the pastor can and ought to do this work.

A thinking pastor thinks of himself as primarily a thinker. With an authentic summons to teach, he teaches people what he thinks about. This is unavoidable. Thus if he thinks primarily about ecclesiastical matters and is afflicted with a thinking disease similar to the disease that eye doctors call "tunnel vision," he teaches the people to think about ecclesiastical matters. He lends his suasive powers to institutional causes. He creates ideas to push toward the people. This stuff comes at them, and they think about organizations, budget, new organ, a couples club, painting the basement, and Aztec jewelry making. A thinking pastor, and every pastor thinks, teaches people by giving his thoughts to them, hoping that they will think too.

But actually we are not concerned here with this kind of thinking, or, more accurately, with these contents. Christian education is our particular concern just now; therefore, the expression "thinking pastor" has got to be defined with more precision: The thinking pastor is a man who thinks about what is going on in the world, who opens himself to the stuff available in books, who conceives of the congregation as a community of scholars, who himself knows the thrill of learning and is consequently ready to live in painful uncertainty as a free, thinking man, and who, above all, sees thinking as a charismatic event. Here is the portrait of a thinking pastor. He makes himself known by the fruits of his thought.

As a project, now, of imagination, put this man in the midst of a congregation. He teaches at all times. His teaching is neither formal nor informal. It is talking to other thinkers and thinking out loud with them. He discovers that the Cadillac dealer has never heard of conspicuous consumption. They begin thinking about Veblen and arguing about whether his idea is not by this late date somewhat archaic. Yet there stand the Cadillacs as background stuff. He visits a lady with terminal cancer; she is too ill to read. So he comes back with a book full of ideas that she is immediately made to think about as he reads to her. A housewife approaches him concerning an article that she has read in a magazine. She awaits his opinion, which he shortly renders—with a flood of bibliographical hints—in such a way that she is laid hold of by new possibilities to think about. At the P.T.A. this thinking man introduces ideas. At the village council he forces thought. At the official board meetings of his church he intrudes on the imaginations of the church officials. He insists by his own intellectual demeanor that the people in his church become intellectually mixed up with modern life. And he does all of this because he is a thinker. No man could organize such activity, any more than he could plan for it to happen. He maintains himself in readiness for what does happen, and greets that procession of new happenings as the place where he must be obedient to God who has thus graced him.

This project of imagination can be misconstrued as an exercise in madness, but only in the event that it does not match expectations of a pastor's role. To the pastor who talks to the Cadillac dealer about the weather, treats the terminal cancer patient as a sad case, the housewife as an exhibitionist, the P.T.A. as a duty, and the official board meeting as an affair to be rigged, then endured, the pastor of the project appears as a madman. Consequently, he is rejected as a model, and furthermore his fundamental understanding of obedience is called into question. Surely many parishioners accustomed to more traditional pastors would reject the thinking pastor as a fraud—unless indirectly they were to become convinced by the thoughtful activity he has occasioned in them that the ostensibly fraudulent behavior was in fact obedient activity. Even rejection is a thoughtful act and does not occur without a painful recognition of the powerful ideological competitor. No matter what comes out of his thinking, the thinking pastor simply thinks, not as an exercise of faith or a proof of faith, but as a venture in faith. In thinking with other people whom he considers thinkers he places his thoughts before them. And they become inevitably faced at least with the possibility of thinking, and perhaps with a charismatic event. The most to be said for those who think of such a man as a madman or an impossible man is that they are probably not very much interested in Christian education.

A thinking church thinks about as many things as there are new events in the lives of every thinker, but it *thinks* about them. It does not devote all of its thinking to the Bible and the Christian religion *because* of its faith. A thinking church worships God corporately. It listens to the rehearsal of its covenant in the Scripture that is read to them. It appropriates the promise of God. It identifies his peculiar godly mode of address. And it finds in the idiom of Scripture and sermon the good news about God. Every true word finds its way into the life of the worshiping people. Each Sunday it is raised from death to life, made new by hearing anew God's word to them. Because of what happens on Sunday, a thinking church is provided with the clues regarding God's grace. It is filled with joy and yet with *angst* at having to return once more from its worship to its life. The church comes under the command of God in its worship and accepts the judgment of that command as good news. Just for the reason that Sunday beckons all the other days of the week toward it, and yet prefers not to intrude into the life of these other incalculably more important days, the church can be a thinking church. It can accept contents for its thought that are furnished by the clues provided on Sunday.

The thinking pastor makes it possible for a church to be a thinking church by making his sermon and Scripture reading authentic Biblical preaching. He awaits the Spirit to provide eyes and ears of faith. The Bible in its language becomes no sacred thesaurus for snappy ideas that the pastor has before he gets to it. It instructs him and nurtures him and forces him to meaningful exposition. Thus the people of God are edified. Here in its rightful place the Bible is accorded its centrality for Christian life and thought. And in its rightful place it becomes a presupposition for the life of thought.

Hearing that Biblical word concerning God, a thinking church believes in him and finds that he is interested in what they do with their days. And also interested in what they think about. Pastors obey the command of God in their sermonizing, in their Scripture reading, but also, and this issues out of the prime obedience, in their recognition of intellectual responsibility. Daniel Jenkins uses the idea of *theatron* to explain this responsibility. He describes the pastor as a kind of theater in which the contemporary intellectual drama takes place. In the concentrated life that he lives in his study he sets himself aside in behalf of the congregation to do what they cannot do. This consists of two activities: the study of the Scriptures and of theology, which tell a preacher how to preach, and the study of the testimonies of the Christian tradition in order to discover how preaching has been done. The second activity is the work of prime thinker and lead reader for the congregation. No one else has this kind of time. The people of the congregation are busy doing their work: selling Cadillacs, keeping house, dying, going to P.T.A. meetings, attending to the official activities of the church, and so on. But the pastor is paid not to be involved in the business world, but to stay in his study in order to build up the people of God.

The pastor's double function leads, however, to one thing. By his preaching and intellectual competence he releases the people of God to live as free, thinking people. He tells them about books and ideas. Inevitably, this is his central commerce with them. Although he encounters resentment, hostility, and, not uncommonly, rejection because he does his work well, he nevertheless drives the people to think, to read, to become informed. The church becomes thus not intellectually respectable—a poor and clumsy goal—but intellectually exciting, holding as many—perhaps more—stimulating charms as the university. It becomes for the people the source of information. It is concerned for their alertness, almost preoccupied over their bigness inside. And in the present day when the whole American world seems dedicated to the emasculation of thought, a thinking church would be a novelty, and, it is thinkable, a corporate charismatic event. Toward such Christian churches Christian education properly works.

"It comes to this," Tarrou said almost casually; "what interests me is learning how to become a saint."

"But you don't believe in God."

"Exactly! Can one be a saint without God?—that's the problem, in fact the only problem, I'm up against today."

A sudden blaze sprang up above the place the shouts had come from and, stemming the wind-stream, a rumor of many voices came to their ears. The blaze died down almost at once, leaving behind it only a dull red glow. Then in a break of the wind they distinctly heard some strident yells and the discharge of a gun, followed by the roar of an angry crowd. Tarrou stood up and listened, but nothing more could be heard.

"Another skirmish at the gates I suppose."

"Well, it's over now," Rieux said.

Tarrou said in a low voice that it was never over, and there would be more victims, because that was in the order of things.

"Perhaps," the doctor answered. "But, you know, I feel more fellowship with the defeated man than with saints. Heroism and sanctity don't really appeal to me, I imagine. What interests me is being a man."

"Yes, we're both after the same thing, but I'm less ambitious."[26]—*Albert Camus.*

[26] Albert Camus, *The Plague* (Alfred A. Knopf, Inc., 1948), pp. 230–231.

Chapter 6

A SMALL UNIVERSITY

The fictional professor of English, Lee Youngdahl, teaches in a fictional West Coast university created by humorist Mark Harris. Harris, in his novel *Wake Up, Stupid,* never goes into Youngdahl's classroom; instead, the professor's teaching is described through the medium of a report of a faculty tenure committee, part of which reads as follows:

Dr. Youngdahl does not show regular clarity of presentation. He does not always address his remarks to the student group, appearing to expect that the student group must accommodate itself to his level. He sometimes addresses his remarks to only a few, and is inclined to be impatient with those whom he considers to be thinking unresponsively. Occasionally he behaves contrarily to demands of a democratic learning experience by shouting at a student, "Wake up, Stupid." . . . There is no evidence of preplanning. Often he appears without books, and seldom with notes, beginning his lesson in a dilatory way, often remarking on the dress or appearance of members of the student group, and one day, observing that a student had dyed her hair, spent a great deal of time that might otherwise have been usefully employed in analyzing her motives. . . .

Dr. Youngdahl's rapport with the student group is excellent. It was amazing to observe that in his discussions he knew all of his students by name, and revealed intimate bits of information concerning them. Although some express dislike for him ("conceited," "arrogant," "aggressive," "relentless," were some of the adjectives employed), the majority liked him. . . .

Dr. Youngdahl has few qualities of leadership. His behavioral example is wholly undesirable. The atmosphere of his classroom is unsocialized, and procedural regularity is lacking. Students often may be seen carrying coffee cups to their seats, and many smoke in violation of prohibitionary signs. One student smoked a cigar. In his views and opinions he is inconsistent, thus affording a formative student group no clear model of attitudinal thought or behavior. In thought and language he is often disrespectful and vulgar, exhibiting a tendency to minimize all the accomplishments of national, civic, or educational institutions, and then in the space of one week reversing his entire position. Students frequently engage in unsupervised debate, as if no discussion leader were available, Dr. Youngdahl merely engaging in this "cross fire," waving his hands and shouting.[27]

Youngdahl turns out to be a remarkably unconventional teacher. He is effective and manifests real competence in the field of English literature (as well as in boxing, letter writing, novel writing, novel adapting, and fathering six children). Effective teachers do not commonly engage in this wide a variety of activities and are not necessarily flamboyant characters whose idiosyncrasies endear them to their amused students. Effective teachers need not have his zeal or energy. But teachers, real teachers like Lee Youngdahl, do lay siege on the conventional poses of the student and attempt to blast him out of his posing into the open. That is, in fact, the natural basic ingredient of teaching. A teacher publicizes his own thought. He exhibits his own thought in the hope that it will bestir the student into thinking. Consequently, he functions as a competitor to the conventions of the *status quo*. He irritates without trying merely to irritate, and stimulates effortlessly, that is, without acting as a stimulant. He surprises his students with thought and gains a reputation with them for being interesting.

In universities the teachers are also scholars, and thus, in making lectures, they are theoretically giving their own thought

[27] Mark Harris, *Wake Up, Stupid* (Alfred A. Knopf, Inc., 1959), pp. 52–55.

to students. This thought, again theoretically, has been measured by accredited academicians against other thought in the
field, so is found to fall within normal professional ranges
of competence. Furthermore, academicians insist that these
teacher-scholars have come to a minimum of general competence in other fields besides the specialty. This is, according to
theory, supposed to ensure interdisciplinary faculty life and,
more important, a well-educated teacher in every classroom.
Each teacher gives his own thought, summarizes the thought
of other scholarly specialists, and instructs the students in fateful matters of style, politics, humor, pathos, manners, and syn-
tax. The student finds an enlarged man before him. He knows
ever after what one acts like. And there generally is one such
man in any university, happily, which is closer to the theory
than most facts come.

When the church was called a "small university" (Chapter
Five) what could have been the intention? The church has no
call to engage a staff of teachers, not of this professional caliber,
at any rate. And surely the churches that do have real teachers
in their membership cannot hope to take them off their real
jobs in order to do without pay what they are already poorly
enough paid to do. If a church were to be constituted as a real
thinking church, these people might think out loud with other
nonprofessional thinkers because that is what the people of
God do, but not in formal, designed, teacher-to-students relationships. And, aside from churches with professional teachers
in the membership, most normal churches just do not have
access to professional teachers. So how can the church without
any teachers become a small university? The problem of
teachers is insuperable. This must be faced squarely.

Contemporary Christian education of adults makes a serious
mistake in assuming that group leaders are teachers. It thus
designs programs for training leaders. (One large denomination calls its program the "Leaders of Leaders" program.) The
assumption of these programs is that the leader of a group
must have practical experience with and insight into the dynamics of group behavior. The major criterion for selecting and

training leaders concerns how sharp they might be in leading groups. But they do *not* have to be experts in any field of intellectual endeavor. If the group discovers that it needs an expert, it calls one in to "resource the group" and then dismisses him.

Leadership problems no longer are insuperable when the greatest difficulty is forthrightly dismissed, namely, of finding teachers who have demonstrated intellectual competence. The churches are full of people who have little of this. There stand the fields of nonexperts, white unto harvest, say the educators no longer interested in teachers. So they have laid in the sickle, to the profound detriment of Christian education.

Martin Buber's two essays "Education" and "The Education of Character" (they appear in *Between Man and Man*) are a source of continual wonderment to the technique-oriented American character. A beautiful passage in the first essay might cause some concern as well as wonderment to the nonexpert-centered leader who is nonetheless billed as an expert in the subtleties of human relations.

> Let us take an example . . . from the drawing class. The teacher of the "compulsory" school of thought began with rules and current patterns. Now you knew what beauty was, and you had to copy it; and it was copied either in apathy or in despair. The teacher of the "free" school places on the table a twig of broom, say, in an earthenware jug, and makes the pupils draw it. Or he places it on the table, tells the pupils to look at it, removes it, and then makes them draw it. If the pupils are quite unsophisticated, soon not a single drawing will look like another. Now the delicate, almost imperceptible and yet important influence begins—that of criticism and instruction. The children encounter a scale of values, that, however unacademic it may be, is quite constant, a knowledge of good and evil that, however individualistic it may be, is quite unambiguous. The more unacademic this scale of values, and the more individualistic this knowledge, the more deeply do the children experience the encounter. In the former instance the preliminary declaration of what alone was right made for resignation or rebellion; but in the latter, where the pupil gains the realization only after he has ventured far out on the way to his achievement, his heart is

drawn to reverence for the form, the educated.

This almost imperceptible, most delicate approach, the raising of a finger, perhaps, or a questioning glance, is the other half of what happens in education.[28]

The teacher of art in this justly famous passage has canons of taste and style. In his subtle way Buber gestures with words toward the imaginative possibility that the teacher was *beyond* merely academic canons. He had come to individualistic knowledge. He was an expert in the ways of lines, tone, shape, relationship, and mood. And if he were not an expert, let us say, not good at art, not even academic, but merely good at human relations, just how would the pupils encounter a scale of values, or a knowledge, as Buber calls it, "of good and evil"? They would not come to know any educated scale or knowledge. And they would thus learn that art does not matter, that it is an excuse for practicing human relations.

The imperceptible raising of a finger, the gesture, the glance, have the great meaning that Buber finds in them because of the educated one who thus gestures. When pupils get only gestures, they are not being educated but subjected to a cruel hoax. When a pupil asks a direct, simple question for information and the teacher responds to the question with, "What do you think?" because the teacher does not know the answer but knows only how to "deal" with this kind of question, we no longer have education but miseducation and mistake.

Skilled leaders are not a priori inexpert teachers. But concentrating ecclesiastical attention on the production of skilled leaders from a general body of people who are not expert enough to teach has meant an alarming increase of leaders and a doubly alarming decrease of teachers. For the church to fulfill its educational ministry, some teachers are required to do the educational jobs. That is why staffing a church with adequate teachers is an insuperable problem, in a way that training leaders is not.

[28] Martin Buber, *Between Man and Man* (The Beacon Press, Inc., 1955), pp. 88, 89.

A Proposal

If the situation were merely hopeless, we could dismiss the whole idea of a thinking church as a small university and return with new zest to ever-bigger building campaigns, bigger budgets, and bigger crowds instead of bigger people—inside. The situation is however, more than hopeless. It is hopeless in regard to doing anything toward constituting a thinking church —as long as traditional, hackneyed gambits are employed. It is hopeless as long as the pastor in coming this far now begins to pull out all his bourgeois paraphernalia of committees, teacher-training sessions, public relations, motivation gimmicks, and so on. It is hopeless to the extent that the pastor as the chief and perhaps only teacher hands off his responsibilities to mere group leaders and gives their groups some new, interesting things to do. But these qualifications of the hopelessness that actually exists do not absolutely condition the situation. Education is still possible in any church if that church is a thinking church and thus appreciates the charismatic nature of education.

My proposal is a concession to sin and a compromise with goals, and I acknowledge this at the very outset. But it is proposed as a possibility for local churches to lay hold of. No promises of immediate or even potential success are mentioned. My proposal calls for the institution of contract groups, so-called because of the manner of their formation and from their opening sessions. (More about these matters in a moment.) The contract group is *ad hoc*. It is a terminal group. It *has* a teacher, but the teacher is a book—or a series of books. Its members listen to the teacher through reading and occasionally meet together for the same reasons that they have to go once in a while to the library. The members apply mutual pressure on one another to fulfill their original "contract." When the obligations of the contract are met, the group disbands.

The most obvious feature of the contract is the end time it specifies. Theodor Reik investigates the relationship of the end and its proleptic power in the course of psychoanalysis. He finds that patients who have to begin acting in the realization that therapy will terminate at such and such a time get into the final stages of analysis much more positively than the patients who think of analysis as a minor-league version of eternal life. This end-time principle supplies intensity and constant hidden pressure on the life of the contract group. It harasses the members with its threat. The terminal date, once accepted, becomes a structural fact.

But does not a school organize its year into quarters and semesters for the same reason? The semester's close is very much in the mind of the student (and the teacher) as it opens. It haunts the proceedings of the class with its realism, the very realism of life: an endless variety, number, and quality of stuff from which selection must be made during a limited, finite time. True, some of the power of the semester's end is vitiated by the fresh semester that stands in the wing. But semesters come in finite, rational numbers, namely, eight, after which, usually, there are no more. So, one way or another, the end is there.

And there should be an end to study, because without the posited end the student suspends himself unrealistically in a sea of possibility—a form of surrender. The professional graduate student offers a case in point. He just goes on and on from degree to degree, playing a listless game against impossible odds. He never can learn everything, and that is the position of a student who cannot foresee a time when he must stop, he must learn everything.

The basic contract is a stated normative quality of study demanded—and accepted. The contract mutually agreed on by its members binds them to the performance of intellectual tasks of a publicly stated and publicly agreed-upon nature. Not only is the content agreed upon but also the style of dealing with the content. The members agree together that they will treat the book (or books) with respect; that they will let its own printed words be the agreed-upon criterion for its own interpretation; that they will not tolerate misrepresentation or

misquotation; that they will aim in their study toward the
fullest possible comprehension of what they agree to study.
Mere verbal assent to these conditioning requirements for contract group membership does not, of course, necessarily mean
that the members are going to be conditioned. But public acceptance along with other contracting members concretely
represents more than mere verbal assent. For the same reasons
young ladies in the moonlight are wary of professions of in-
finite love from their lovers. They sensibly want to know
whether that profession can be made before witnesses, in public, and out loud. For the same reasons orthodox Freudian
analysts ask their patients to lie down on the couch, to associate
with as much freedom as they are capable of, not to change
their marital state, and so on, during the course of analysis. The
patient who agrees is thereafter stuck with his own public
declaration.

Let us imagine such a situation as this. A thinking pastor
discovers some thinking people in his church. *He* decides that
some section of the church should, as an evangelical witness,
begin serious thinking about, let us say, psychiatry (although
it could be the new-style sociology represented by Edgar Fried-
enberg and Paul Goodman, the nineteenth-century American
novel, the postwar novel, the poems of Ogden Nash, the income
tax, city planning, *Mad* magazine, or Augustine's *De Trinitate*,
etc.). He does some thinking on his own, in private and in
consultation with expert experts. Now he decides upon a list
of books that will present the central ideological features of
psychiatry—as a scientific and cultural phenomenon—or is it
movement? He settles on Freud's *New Introductory Lectures
on Psychoanalysis*, Jung's *Psychology of the Unconscious*, gives
a choice between Otto Rank's *Will Therapy; and, Truth and
Reality* and Otto Fenichel's *The Psychoanalytic Theory of
Neurosis*, and concludes with Harry Stack Sullivan's *The In-
terpersonal Theory of Psychiatry*. These books represent the
possibility for serious thinking about a serious subject. He goes
then to thinking people, privately. He tells each one what is
on his mind and inquires into his willingness to do this study

under the elaborated terms. They express interest. They come to the original contract meeting. Here the pastor spells out the contract. Each member pledges himself in agreement with the terms of the contract to do the outlined study. After every member has made his public agreement the group gets down to its central business, namely, of going out of the door to private houses for private study.

During private study the individual member comes to know the teacher, which is the book. He reads the whole book as an entity and thinks the thoughts of the author. For the moment the thoughts of no one else matter. The teacher is given freedom to say what he will, and the reader devotes himself to the simple act of understanding often incredibly difficult concepts. As an aid to understanding he talks out loud, writes statements down, and asks questions. Finally, now, he begins to see the wholeness. At the next group session (the test session) he has abundant opportunity to discover whether or not he has in truth understood the text, because his fellows are also going to be at the session and they too will have read the book.

The test session becomes a clearinghouse for the ideas in the books. According to the contract, the text itself is the teacher and its own best interpreter, so questions of meaning that arise between members can be resolved only by the text, not by loud shouting or moving for consensus. Because the great and famous author-thinker is dead and in all probability would not come to the meeting even if he were alive, and also because no other teachers are available, the book itself must do this kind of teaching as the group members test themselves publicly on their understanding. Often people learn a great deal from tests as they flunk and as they do well.

The life of the contract group alternates between private reading and public testing at a pace predetermined by the end time, and with a teacher whose intellectual gestures and syntactical aplomb offer to the privileged student a scale of values and a knowledge of the teacher as an educated man. What comes out of such study? A number of people who are informed because they have thought. The project of the group is to come out at just this point. The students have nothing to give immediately to the church, in the way of reports or advice; they have learned nothing directly about the Christian faith. These results seem rather skimpy compared to ordinary adult study that goes on and on and can be reasonably expected to produce teachers for other parts of the Sunday school, alert Bible believers who know what to do with their daily lives, and so on. Compared to the results envisioned by the new look in adult education, contract group results are inconclusive and much too specified in terms of verbal-rational skill goals. Indeed, these results are, on purpose, inconclusive, and they are specified in the only legitimate goals that education can conceive: verbal-rational skills.

The contract group—what it thinks and the way it thinks— embodies the belief that God has graced the intellectual areas of spiritual (hidden) life. Here is one place where God has dealings with man as surely as he does in market, office, gas station, or before the television set. Such a belief grows out of the simple evangelical conviction of God's saving work. It happens in the mind and its conceptual activities if anywhere at all. Phenomenologies of salvation are impossible to write now as ever, but if one were to be written, it would be framed in words, organized in paragraphs and chapters, that is, it would appear in a conceptual garb, presupposing the life of the mind, whether the phenomenology dealt with it or not. Proposing other areas that are indigenously charismatic does not alter the reality of *this* area, which happens to be the area in which Bible, theology, and preaching fall. The goal of an informed laity need never be apologized for as an impractical activity. Its realization will prove decisive for the Protestant Church while such practical activities as stewardship tub-thumping or indoctrinating all the families of the parish in the arts of family worship merely sink it deeper in idolatry.

As surely as the contract group projects conceptual work, it runs into trouble. The average thinker in the Protestant Church has few conceptual skills and even these are not well developed. The trouble consists of dealing with significant (potentially charismatic?) books before the thinkers have the skills to deal with them. The reader labors over concepts as such and this labor is often doubled by unfamiliarity with vocabulary. Allusions are often mystifying. But here the reader is paying for a misspent youth and/or an inept high school education. The contract group as such cannot rule out the poorly educated. And restricting membership to college graduates would prove a great disappointment as well as a perpetuation of one of the grandest lies in American life: that the college diploma guarantees reading skills. American adults in general do not read well, a national trait that goes hand in hand with disdain of explicitly intellectual activities.

But the unavoidable trouble is in itself educational. In going at a painfully slow pace through a big book, the reader must remain close to the printed page. He knows the luxury of watching the creation of ideas at essentially the same speed of their composition and thus learns indirectly how the author's mind works. Moreover, he learns not to be intimidated. A big idea is made up of a great many little words as well as the polysyllabic monsters.

"Sticking to the text" has no a priori distinction as a Protestant idea. It comprehends the difficulties and great wickedness of the reader and calls for his continual repentance. Therefore it has merit for the Protestant. Radical openness to the future includes openness to the particular words that are filling the eyes of the reader. The words are perhaps opaque to him. But does he therefore skip them? Or if they are clear, does he agree or disagree with a haste that betrays misunderstanding? His mode of life as Christian man should predispose a humility and patience before the text of a book. The mode of the contract group consequently looks for the trouble of hard labor and cultivates respect for the text. In such ways the mind of the reader is enlarged and instructed. After textual labor the reader can test his work and range outward from the text to the implications that it posits for curious and imaginative thought. But not before. Close attention to the text gives the clues for imagination anyway. Hence, within the underlying contract of the study lies the authentic Protestant witness to intellectual integrity.

I have chosen the study of psychiatry to describe the characteristics of the contract group when I might as well have used a dozen other subjects that call for such study. Why psychiatry? Because it is a difficult study. If a group of high school graduates can understand this material, it can deal with almost anything. I am convinced that it *can* deal with almost anything, including the study of psychiatry. The difficulty of the material was not the only reason. That reason alone could lead to the study of many conceptually difficult subjects, such as the theory of numbers. What would commend the study of the theory of numbers to the people of God? It is theoretically conceivable, but under conditions that enlightened imagination has yet to come upon. No, the study of psychiatry has compelling features other than its difficulty. It appears in popular psychologizing articles as an omniscient savior of mankind. It has been embraced by numberless clergymen who delight in blending psychology and religion. The church stands first in awe, then in dread, of psychiatry, but without knowing very much about the subject. Aside from the caricature with which it is confronted, the church has little firsthand acquaintance with the subject.

Yet, behold what veritable miracles psychiatry performs every day! Consider the importance of the psychiatrist to industry, to advertising, to our courts, hospitals, schools, and churches. And consider further the sad fact that truncated versions of the thought basic to psychiatry are about all the medical layman ever sees. Yet, like persons of other intellectual disciplines, psychiatrists produce books and pamphlets by the thousands, and undoubtedly feel guilty if they do not keep moderately up to date. When a representative of the psychiatric community attempts to interpret for medical laymen the internal structure of psychiatric thought, does he tell them about this forefront with its new developments? He does not. He discourses condescendingly, as if to not very bright children. The development of psychiatric understanding of man could easily turn out to be the most impressive achievement of the entire Western age. Or, it could cloak the most recent appearance of the devil! Must Christians wait for psychiatry to give the answer? Must Christians put up with insipid discussions of the relationship of psychology and religion, the appearance of God in which legitimatizes everything except the headache? Christians can no longer avoid their serious responsibility to find out what is going on in this sector of modern life, and they will discover nothing until they perform the honest work of scholars.

This kind of study is a venture of faith and not a study of faith. If it were to become a study of faith, it would become sterile. It dodges the issues by retreating into a stifling cultic closeness. It baptizes Sigmund Freud or excoriates him with the same magic words, "Jesus Christ," but without hearing whether Sigmund Freud speaks the words of truth or the words of sin. Ignazio Silone has one of his magnificent anticlerical heroes speak the following lines in the novel *Bread and Wine:*

> In times of conspiratorial and secret struggle the Lord is obliged to hide himself and assume pseudonyms. Besides, and you know it, he does not attach very much importance to his name; on the contrary, at the very beginning of his commandments he ordained that his name should not be taken in vain. Might not the ideal of social justice that animates the masses today be one of the pseudonyms the Lord is using to free himself from the control of the churches and the banks?[29]

This surprising reflection breathes Biblical realism. Into which underground might God have now gone, there to perform among men what he has determined to do? Thus faith realistically listens for his word at all times, in all places.

What now if faith ventures to study the historical contents of the Christian faith, not as an automatic reaction or a pious stance but as an intellectual questing? Is it possible to study the Bible? Might a contract group accept Bible study as a

[29] Ignazio Silone, *Bread and Wine,* translated from the Italian by Gwenda David and Eric Mosbacher (Harper & Brothers, 1957), p. 241.

project? Surely it *might*, if it understood what it was doing and how the contents of this study are uniquely related to the life of the members. Numerous objections to Bible study have been raised throughout this book just because the direction and atmosphere of the study reveal that the unique relationship between content of study and life of member has not been understood. Edward Farley's ingenious remarks on the lay theology might give us some insight here.

> [The] grain of truth in lay theology helps clarify the bushel of danger in antitheology. The antitheologians, it seems, want to be "religious" without being theological. They want to be "Christian businessmen," devoted pastors, and ardent teachers, without splitting theological hairs. Problems are raised here concerning the implied view of the nature of theology and also the nature of being "Christian." Apparently they are identifying theology with the highly technical work of theological specialists. It is understandable that they comprehend or appreciate little of these technical endeavors. Our point, however, is that theology refers to the something broader than esoteric scholarship. Theology is also the kind of questioning or inquiring into a problem which questions from the Word. It is the attempt to live under the Word by raising the intellectual question of the nature and content of the Word.[30]

Bible study by laymen cannot be a searching for the Word or an expression of reverence for the Word. Both these activities are undertaken outside the church. But it can, as Farley suggests, be an intellectual questioning of the nature and content of the Word, as this questioning is related to the key document in the history of that people to whom God has spoken.

At any rate, if undertaken rightly, the Bible has got to be accorded the thoughtful attention given to other books. This is made difficult because of the spirited approval typically rendered the Book, but not impossible. Thinking adults in serious study will have to attend to the Book as such and thus to its vexing questions of authorship, dependable text, character and

[30] Edward Farley, "Professional and Lay Theology," *Theology Today* (April, 1960), pp. 37–38.

style of the multiplicity of its materials, central events, and so on. Some curious adults might tackle Wellhausen before Noth, Alt, and Eichrodt, but how could serious students avoid the questions or the thoughtful answers to be found in the work of these men? Some curious adults might also find that Bultmann's vast project of demythologizing the Bible has the ingredients of a working answer to most of the hard questions that they have raised countless times. The point is that, as thinkers, the students must devote their thinking to the matters that are raised for questioning. As a contract group the students are obligated to treat the text with honesty and respect. Having a life under the Word of God and aware of its summons to readiness for the new, the students listen here as elsewhere for its authentic cadences, at precisely the same time that they raise the question of authenticity. It becomes message, history, proclamation, cultic teacher, and ancient literature all at once, because in serious study this is what the Bible simultaneously is.

Students I have known generally prefer the Old Testament the more both Testaments are studied. They prefer its superior literary quality. Second Isaiah or the Samuel-Kings corpus rate with anything in ancient literature. It is "great stuff." Once opened before intellectual activity, the Old Testament discloses its brilliance. And this rather fascinates the student, probably because of the discordances sounding in his depths over what he once upon a time so arrogantly assumed the Old Testament to be. If the Old Testament gains intellectual respect, the New Testament proves to be a disappointment. Among the New Testament Gospels and letters only the Fourth Gospel has literary merit as such, i.e., structure, style, considered use of language, elegant metaphors, elaborate interlacing of themes, etc. Also, the New Testament leaves too many important matters up in the air, such as the disposition of the dead, the ambiguous relation of law and gospel, shifting Christology, multiple definitions of faith, ambivalence toward Jewish apocalypse, and inability to locate John the Baptist always at the same place within the holy history.

Somehow it seems perfectly fitting for well-dressed, well-fed, nicely manicured Americans to devote their intellectual energies to the study of the Old Testament. But a certain anomaly can be found in these same people *studying* the letters of Paul. Not that the letters are inferior. They are so white-hot! The anomaly is not lost on American students. They can become profoundly uneasy in the spiritual presence of that hungry, ugly, and egotistical little Jew. (This picture accounts for Paul's disfavor among American Protestants more than his supposed variance with the "sweet" Gospels.) Students are shaken by this study; they are intellectually accosted by the material, affronted, and made to see the insistence of God in his determination to restore the creation to its rightful glory. For many students the letters of Paul are the last straw as well as the last item of Biblical study. The Word of God makes whole all-the-way sense, for the first time.

Not unusually, serious lay Bible students become devoted critics of the present-day church. They criticize the preaching, church organization, celebration of the sacraments, choice of anthems, decisions of official boards, Sunday school, youth program, and about anything that happens. This is not a critical spirit. It is a reflection of the fact that they have become lay theologians (in Farley's broad sense). They bring the whole life of the church beneath the Word. Nothing can maintain itself in their eyes as an autonomous activity that needs no judgment or life from the Word since it has its authorization from tradition. While the appearance of lay theologians on the scene of some churches would be a cause of consternation rather than rejoicing, the possibility of their eventual appearance is formed when study of the nature of the Word is begun. Honest study, particularly of the New Testament, represents an existential affront to the whole of modern life, not just to the church. The student learns the presuppositions for any of his study. Venturing in faith, he who contracts to study the contents of faith is freed the more to undertake future ventures that God commands. Or, to employ a Kierkegaardian figure, readiness repeats itself: that is true Bible study.

Onward—*Mort Sahl*

Chapter 7

THE STORY OF THE
LONELY INDIVIDUAL

When contract groups have disbanded, study groups have become obsolete, and newer groups have crumbled before the newer design of yet newer generations of experts, the lonely individual will be as lonely as ever. Faith as a venturing is a meaningful category only for him. Since identified so memorably—and with such shocking intimacy—by Sören Kierkegaard over one hundred years ago, he has haunted, mocked, or retreated from the trends and countertrends of ecclesiastical life. His awesome subjectivity has never been appropriately managed. Although willing to join with the others in intellectual sport, he soon turns recalcitrant on them. Pliable to the stresses of socialized life, he goes on its parties and laughs riotously, indeed, often proving to be the life of the party, but always to return into his subjectivity, there at times to contemplate suicide. At prayers he tries his best, but the voice of subjectivity does not silence itself, nor will it be silenced by cold glances. He cannot pray with the others. He is not, after all, the others; he is merely himself alone.

Modern ecclesiastical theology has not taken proper account of him in speaking of him as a person or asserting his unique

135

individuality. His true marks are not to be described *in medias res*. He is not, for instance, a "person" or an individual who glides in and out of various groupings. He is quite himself all by himself in a loneliness that per se defies description. If he were not lonely, that is, if he were a happy, gregarious creature, then Christian education could go along at a merry clip. But instead it halts and sputters and stalls because in dealing with groups it finds *the lonely individual*. Christian education is perennially at his mercy, no matter what transpires on the ecclesiastical front.

Let me illustrate. Radical experiments in churchcraft are being performed in Europe and now in America. They are allied to a brilliantly eclectic theology composed of equal parts of Bonhoeffer, Barth, and Kraemer. Their aim seems to be the development of new ecclesiastical structures that are specifically indigenous to the modern, rather than to the nineteenth-century, world. The individual experiments differ widely. But they hold in common a newly recovered sense of the *laos Theou*. The motto of this development goes as follows: the mission of the people of God is to live in the world and minister there to the world's existential nature, but ministering nonetheless as true men and not as religious freaks. The experiments attempt, then, to facilitate the ministry by encouraging study of the world. The Protestant monastic order in Taizé, Switzerland, maintains a structure of devotion, work in the secular order, and study. The Agape community in Turin, Italy, seeks to provide for the villagers or city dwellers of that nation a place to which they can come in order to wrestle with the meaning of their life or any life. Similar lay study centers have been established at Parishfield, Michigan, and the Faith and Life community located at Austin, Texas. These are fundamentally places designed for the contemplation of the Christian faith and its relation to American life in momentary and meaningful abstraction from it.

These experiments have strong anticlerical notions and are distinctly antiecclesiastical. They radiate good and almost cheerful destructiveness. Together they might, eventually, break down the huge bureaucratic bourgeois monolith bearing the name Protestant Church. That seems to be their professed business. An ecumenical theologian now teaching that subject in Princeton Seminary has written a rather representative book for the—shall we call it a—movement. Its title, *Outside the Camp*, proceeds from Heb. 13:12–14: "So Jesus also suffered outside the gate in order to sanctify the people through his own blood. Therefore let us go forth to him outside the camp, bearing abuse for him. For here we have no lasting city." It avows a total reappraisal of the church in mission to the world, not the church down on the corner—the St. John's by the gas station—but the *laos Theou* in the *cosmos*.[31] The internal temperature of the movement that Mr. West writes for is high. But the record-high temperature to date is held by Paul Van Buren. His article "The New Biblical Theology in Parish Life" is a simply devastating attack on the institutional American church.[32] The paint on the walls of the church is blistered these days by many comparable, though more restrained, utterances.

Unorganized younger theologians in virtually every American seminary carry the anti-institutional good news to each fresh crop of seminarians. The younger theologians are perhaps the most important figures in the movement. They prosecute their case with vigor and intellectual passion before budding young theologues who may one day get in the mood to revolt and in one cataclysmic effort break through the oppressive tyrannies of overorganized, bureaucratized institutionalism. That possibility grows more definite each year.

But the movement, were it to accomplish its breakthrough, would thus be obligated to establish new structures consonant with its new understanding of the church as *laos Theou* in the *cosmos*. It would have to have preachers and seminaries; it would consequently have to have an offering of money; it would have to study and train the young. No matter how thrill-

[31] Charles West, *Outside the Camp* (Doubleday & Co., Inc., 1959).
[32] Paul Van Buren, "The New Biblical Theology in Parish Life," *Religion in Life* (Autumn, 1959).

ing the prospects are for a new day in the American Protestant Church, even if it amounts to a new Reformation, some of these people in the *laos Theou* are going to have to attend to the teaching. And when they do, they will encounter just who they are faced with right now in his pre-new-Reformation state: the lonely individual.

The teaching situation does not seem to change very much. The patterns of his existence are cut from the cloth of a particular age, his mores dictated by official consensus, but the lonely individual from century to century lives on in unrivaled privacy. He welcomes knowledge but resists challenge. He comes to love the halfway house of the dilettante and eventually settles there instead of in the scorner's seat or in the place of the righteous. Skeptical of the practical workings together of people, he nonetheless carries a fantastically unskeptical fancy within him that one day, somehow, he will be happy, contented, and reveling in the luxury of whatever the opposite of loneliness is. The perceptible gulf between his fancy and his incapacities even to name the opposite of his loneliness goes unappraised. He can believe absolutely anything if he wants to: that Hitler is a fine young god; that Negroes are an inferior race; that black is white; that Bridey Murphy lived in the eighteenth and the twentieth centuries; that sex and love are distinct experiences; that the world is flat; that America is the best country in world history. But he need believe nothing in itself. He is skeptical of everything but also given to self-indulging gullibility. As such he is a foolish and sinful man, more ignorant than brave, and braver than to lose himself to the others. Is it not amusing to discover in this great age of conformity that not one individual *thinks of himself* as a conformist? When individually questioned, individuals uniformly resist the notion that they are conformists, although they agree that everyone else is. Yea, all is indeed vanity and a striving for wind.

Yet this is the lonely individual, and the true business of Christian education is to teach this man to think and to provide some clues that will lead him to think responsibly as a

Christian man. In Chapter Six we mentioned the fact that contract groups are a concession to sin and a compromise with goals. Now perhaps the import of that statement can be worked out. Fundamentally, such a statement reminds us, the Christian community has not gathered to itself a group of brilliant, creative, stimulating, thoughtful people. Neither its clergy nor its laity displays particularly outstanding intellectual gifts. Its members—each one, finally, a lonely individual in his own rightful being—prefer minimum intellectual effort to hard work. Each steadily keeps the pressure off himself as much as he can. Many influences have subtly led him to think of himself with growing concreteness (i.e., with the facts to prove it), as a low thinker, one whose mind goes flitting off the subject at the least diversion. His thoughts seem too trifling, and so on.

Today's Christian education has inherited a legacy that privately dismayed educators of the past, namely, the necessity for contriving situations that will *force* this lonely individual to think. The reason for having any kind of group lies in the constitution of the lonely individual. He must be prodded, stimulated, urged on to do what he tends by himself to avoid. The contract group takes these structural factors seriously and offers a way of keeping the pressure on. And we are not talking now about man who has *no* future that he sees opening graciously before him. We are talking about Christian man, whose life has been forgiven and is daily made new. *This* man forces the concession to sin because although faithful he is yet sinful and although venturing, he is nonetheless ignorant. Distrust lurks in his every trusting gesture. *He* wills not to think and consequently must be badgered into a situation where he gives his word before others, and thus having pledged himself, keeps at what he should normally be able to procrastinate over indefinitely.

Furthermore, the contract group concedes that the lonely individual will continue lonely until his death. Such capacities as he does own for being stirred up or absorbed must be respected but not misunderstood. These are passive, not active, capacities. Existentially shy, he does not go out to other individuals easily. Love for this reason is more than meeting. It is a monumental achievement.

His shyness is in evidence to quite the same degree before books, articles, or hard speeches. That is why the advertisers have been having a field day with him during the past decade. They have blessed his passivity, appealed to it, driven him into yet deeper shyness, and have magnified the problems of the very people who are forcing in on him with enticements that might excite him into exertive intellectual activity.

This concession to sin, however, concedes the sin to each individual—one by one. It recognizes that the Christian community one by one defaults its responsibilities for ministry in the world. It sees that corporate guilt is shared, but one after another of its members are the guilty ones. One by one, also, the Christian community is taught. It learns to read and to think one by one. The group character of the Christian community finally turns out to be an illusion productive of the greatest possible amounts of mischief. Groupings are *ad hoc* concessions precisely to the basic constitution of the church as a *community* of lonely individuals, whose very community testifies to their loneliness and individuality. So groupings are arranged for tentatively, in a spirit half whimsical and half dreadful—the dread springing out of the possibility that the lonely individual will retreat yet farther into himself. The contract group attempts to actualize the dread and the whimsey. It makes explicit—in its time limit, in its silent teacher, and in the large amounts of lonely studious work it provides for—that the group does not study but that individual students are grouped for essentially bibliographical purposes.

Concessions to persistence of sin in the life of the believer have in the proposal of the contract group been yoked to compromises with goals, as we have indicated. The goal of Christian education is simply the education of Christians. But the simplicity is deceptive. A Parkinsonian kind of law could be framed to cover the situation in terms such as these: ease of statement is in inverse proportion to ease of execution. This goes for the convicted criminal no less than for Christian

education. The goal is so nicely and roundly stated. It is em-
broidered with no frills or filled with precise qualifiers. Yet its execution is tormented by the most extraordinary difficulties. Perhaps nice hard goals are in the long run better appreciated by
churchmen who have the wit to realize that the hard goals do
not require as much work as the easy ones. But we have little
choice in the selection of goals. They are more or less given
to us. Our area of choice exists in how much we are willing
to compromise them.

The contract group proposal embodies a severe compromise.
If the words "education" and "Christian" are taken at their full
value, then individual, spontaneous study is called for which
bears the characteristics of venturing, painful uncertainty,
openness to *anything*, and so on. Such study should not have
to be arranged for. It should be provoked by hearing the
preached word and appropriating the sacramental word. Having heard the word of God, Christian man should live in sensitive anticipation for the word of God on the frontier of his
life where the future comes into his present. But regardless
now of what should happen, it obviously does not. Christian
man goes to sleep during the sermon prepared as likely as not
on "spiritual values in a materialistic age" or other irrelevant
Gnostic dainties. Christian man does not even plunge into passionate and devoted study following faithful preaching. He
loafs or watches television. Bored Christian man (of the female
species, American) might more willingly drop everything in
order to study, but, on the whole, gadgeteering Christian man
(of the male species, American) has small enthusiasm for
books.

The goal for Christian education therefore immediately
brings into mind the ideal means for achieving the goal: one
teacher for every student. Less ideal means might be one
teacher for every five or at the most ten students. But whatever
can Christian education do with only one teacher in all likelihood and a whole congregation of dilatory students? It can
compromise its notion of education. And that is what the contract group embodies.

The compromise, however, attempts to come as close to the goal as seems presently possible. Much lonely study and excellent teachers are made possible by the contract group. But after these commendatory remarks have been entered into the record, the dilatory tactics of the individual student must be considered from the vantage point of the compromise as a phenomenon worthy of careful attention. The thinking man has a loneliness and a privacy that forbids solid, difficult thought in all but the smallest possible time segments. He thinks about himself so much of the time that he does not have a lot of time to spare for the world or the community or the Word of God. That is precisely the point where contract groups fall short educationally. The lonely individual is an interminable thinker-about-himself.

A pietistic tradition has tricked the Christian public with some semimagical exegesis into believing that concern for "self," i.e., "self-ishness," or "self-love," must be dealt with firmly and gotten rid of as soon as possible. Certainly the motivation is winsome, but the exegesis is terrible, and the chances of replacing selfishness with selflessness are nil. The most spectacular example of selfishly stumping for the banishment of selfishness is furnished by the stumpers themselves. Their impassioned sermons display prominent marks of self-worthiness, self-esteem, self-concern, self-bettering things such as raw-silk suits, golden trumpets, steak dinners after the stumping, and then to bed, but not before a bit of mutual admiration. What is commonly called "selfishness" does not just wilt under the heat of denunciation. What could be a more curious phenomenon than an utterly private, lonely individual passionately pursuing the question throughout his whole being of whether or not he is selfish?

The self cannot be denied or, furthermore, be pushed aside in education or in anything else. The self in its interior characteristic activity manifests a constant caring for itself, an endless consideration for and fascination with itself. Carl Jung provides in the following quotation a startling confirmation of what each individual has surely come to recognize inside himself. Not self-love but self-disgust is the authentic inward condition of the self.

> We cannot change anything unless we accept it. Condemnation does not liberate, it oppresses. I am the oppressor of the person I condemn, not his friend and fellow sufferer. I do not in the least mean to say that we must never pass judgment in the cases of persons whom we desire to help and improve. . . .
> Perhaps this sounds very simple, but simple things are always the most difficult. In actual life it requires the greatest discipline to be simple, and the acceptance of oneself is the essence of the moral problem and the epitome of the whole outlook upon life. That I feed the hungry, that I forgive an insult, that I love my enemy in the name of Christ—all these are undoubtedly great virtues. What I do unto the least of my brethren, that I do unto Christ. But what if I should discover that the least amongst them all, the poorest of all the beggars, the most impudent of all the offenders, the very enemy himself—that these are within me, and that I myself stand in the need of the alms of my own kindness—that I myself am the enemy who must be loved—what then? As a rule, the Christian's attitude is then reversed; there is no longer any question of love or long-suffering; we say to the brother within us "Raca," and condemn and rage against ourselves. We hide it from the world; we refuse to admit ever having met this least among the lowly in ourselves. Had it been God himself who drew near to us in this despicable form, we should have denied him a thousand times before a single cock had crowed.[33]

This sort of consideration places the matter of the self in constant attendance upon itself in a different frame of reference. Indeed, the individual in the depths of his individuality is a thoughtful being and must by his very constitution contemplate the stuff that comes at him, *but* in such a way that *self-contemplation* runs along a parallel track simultaneously. This concern for oneself that has traditionally been found horrid by traditional piety—and much orthodox theology—

---

[33] C. F. Jung, *Modern Man in Search of a Soul,* cited in *Man and God,* compiled by Victor Gollancz (Houghton Mifflin Company, 1951), pp. 234, 235.

can certainly become horrid and a veritable hell. But it also is the only scene there is for the enactment of the educational drama.

Consider that while hard at work in the study of a remarkably important book, a woman might also be *thinking* for the one hundred thousandth time in her life that her calves are really not full enough. Or imagine a man equally hard at work on an equally important book stolidly remembering a time in his youth when he fell out of a rowboat. This goes on in hard study all the time. Even the utterly absorbed, creative involvement of the student in his task evokes from him a constant glowing pleasure that amounts to a recognition of his involvement—a delight that can "almost be tasted." Educators do not ordinarily deal extensively with the constant asides that the reader makes to himself that are not apropos of the text. If this waste time were to be filled, ten or maybe twenty times the reading done by the most conscientious student could be accomplished. Now, of course, there is the question: Is the reader, when he is merely contemplating his leg or remembering a forgotten errand or chastising himself for a non-bon mot made in a conversation, wasting time?

According to educational goals—and this holds for Christian education—the thinker is wasting his time. That is why the contract group proposal is a recognized compromise of the goal. Since the church cannot provide one teacher in constant attendance on every student in order to keep him at work, he will dally with seductively nonstudious material. Tradition prompts a despairing sigh over this activity, new motivational gimmicks, or, perhaps, more slickly written prose. But the time-wasting student should not be despised for his self-absorption. By no means. His very care for himself should be seized upon, greeted with kisses, rings, a fatted calf, and great merriment.

What traditionally goes under the banner of dilatory tactics employed by the lazy thinker incapable of concentration is—thinking! Christian education is concerned with thinking. Why not this thinking-about-oneself? Nothing seems likely to be gained by devising ever more subtle and ingenious means to get around the thinker. The contract groups stumble just there, as do all groups. Yet the realism in which contract groups have been proposed, that is, in consideration of the compromise that the proposal embodies, points toward a new understanding of what makes the compromise necessary. As ally to, co-operator with, and friend of, contract-group-type thinking, thinking-about-oneself should be made a permanent part of the adult educational scene. A thinking church can bolster the lonely individual in his contemplation of the inner contents of his own life. To that end a final proposal is hereby advanced, which is:

The Study of Fiction

Frank Yerby, a writer of mildly combustible romantic adventure stories, defends his particular kind of story by pointing out that he attempts to relieve the "thundering, crashing boredom of the common man." Yerby sells well enough and writes nicely and smoothly, but he has missed the common man by a full ten yards with that shot about his boredom. The common man may be oppressed by the world situation, depressed about himself, nagged by worry, harried by unbidden thoughts concerning his inconsequential place in life, and so on. But he should never be called "bored." He buys a Yerby yarn precisely because he should like to retreat a while from a situation that has grown too hot. The retreat principle unfortunately accounts for what few books are sold by the fiction industry today, and thus should not be denigrated with unkind remarks. But authors who abet the retreat tendency by writing fiction designed and advertised as suitable retreat fare should be dropped from the union or accorded some other punishment.

Fiction enjoys no good reputation with the American public just because it has recognized that fiction has no weight or consequence. It can be used instead of or along with alcohol or Miltown to dull the ache of strictly inside, private, lonely individuality. As a tested guess, seven out of any ten books leading the best seller lists at any given time will prove to be poor stories, slickly written, hopped up with deliberately induced erotic materials, featuring unlikely characters in unlikely conclusions to tales that should never have been told. The average nonfiction reader shows much good sense in staying away from this stuff. But he should not be left in a state of doubt over the wider area of fiction that comprehends some stories that he would find fascinating.

Without engaging in a hassle with stated authorities over suitable criteria for evaluating fiction, thus establishing examples of categorical "bests," "goods," and "ordinaries," we might for the moment consider one criterion suitable to our purposes. *If a story captivates the reader, it is a good story for the reader to read.* That fundamentally is the conclusion reached by the stated authorities anyway, although struck off in measurably more glossy language. For the reader to lose himself, a feat impossible, by definition, for him to perform, means that he has become totally absorbed in a story. The reader does in fact forget himself for the moment. He lays himself aside as uninteresting because he has become interested in something else. For a few moments he becomes a huge eye and nothing else. His activities become mechanical functions in serving the eye, much as in sleep the body twists and adjusts itself in efforts to accommodate the sleeping conscious mind. The hours fly. And when he has finished his story, for it now belongs to him by virtue of his having read it, he cannot easily bring himself to think about the pedestrian matters that had concerned him before he began the story. He is actually still in his story, thinking about it. Very slowly and often reluctantly he returns to these practical affairs of his life. Maybe he will catch himself remembering that story weeks or years later, and even on his deathbed.

Could not a Yerby romance do just as well as a Kafka masterpiece in captivating the reader? Not just as well, not if the reader is rendered his true weighty importance in the matter of his own captivation. He does not, to be frank, find

Yerby very convincing. Yerby is good at make-believe men and women who make love in far-away places. Therefore he does evoke a certain wistfulness in the reader who says as he reads on, "If only it were true." Kafka is good, however, in a far different way. He writes stories that are like *almost* nightmarish dreams already in progress, to the contents of which a reader is invited to attend. And the reader must furnish the wonder. Joseph K. is a blurred figure who can be a psychosexual figure for the unconscious mind of the reader, a wandering pilgrim, a guilty man, a lonely individual, Franz Kafka himself in masked autobiographical dress, or a shadow of the reader. And the story of Joseph K., concerning a trial, can be a psychosexual drama, a story of pilgrimage, a parable of guilt and redemption, and a story of the plight of the lonely individual. No one reads this story saying, "If only it were true." Rather, he asks, "Is it true?" and is immediately seized by misgivings or disgust, the valence of which should not be misinterpreted.

To have the capacity to captivate, a story must deny wistfulness at the outset and instruct the reader in the story itself as an engrossing elaboration of the life of paper people. Everything in the author will have had to be sacrificed to the story he has created if the reader can be expected to put away his internal occupations in order to read the story. The paper people may be representations of the author or of flesh-and-blood people he has known, but once in a story their origins count for little. What do they do? say? feel? And then what happens? Where does it all come out? True-to-life stories are not stories. True-to-stories stories are the only stories that really captivate.

With as much reserve as I can muster, I should like to propose that an educated Christian man can be characterized by the stories he thinks about. A story, in its simple form, begins, runs into complexity, and ends. A story supplies to the thinking individual a clear picture of what in *his* story lie in the shadowy regions of mystery and wonder: his beginning and his end. His preoccupation with the pressing nowness of his own life is tainted with confusion and doubt because he has no clear pictures about his yesterday or his tomorrow. His absorption in a story bears mute testimony to his anxiety over this present *today*, for in a story he will know how the matter turns out, whereas he will never know his own tomorrow. In the story he sees how the complexity is worked through or how it triumphs over the hero. He can observe the inner characteristics of decision, and the measureless depths of tangled motives that produce a decision. He sees how it is with life and thus takes the story into himself and his life—as a part of the how it is with his own life.

A willfully ignorant man is also arrogant. He defiantly says that he knows about life—on the basis of his own thinking about life. He repudiates the grace of his own past by ignoring it or resisting the disguised messages that it brings. He turns against his own future, and its grace, with the fanatic zeal of an empire builder—or a schizophrenic. No story is worth his time. He is blocked both ways, so that in effect he has neither past nor future. If he is a businessman, then he measures each day by the receipts of the day, if she is a housewife by the perfection with which the scheduled activities have gone off, and so on. The day in itself in all of the thinking it has occasioned occupies the lonely, blocked individual exclusively.

The educated man, however near his life may be to the life of the hipster or his square brother and sister, has a hidden storylike life. He lives much nearer Prometheus, Tom Jones, Jude, Temple Drake, Seymour, or Captain Ahab. By their light he has clarified somewhat the penumbra of mystery that surrounds his today. And if he is Christian man, he stands ready to accept the gracious tokens that proceed from God and to risk his life under the command of God.

Much that is compromised by the contract group can be recouped by planting in front of the thinking Christian man a never-ending flood of possibly captivating fiction. For this no groups are necessary, no arranging need be planned. A teacher performs few more powerful acts than suggesting books to read. Nowhere does he make those indefinably edu-

cative gestures with such deftness as he does when telling of
a story that he has found wonder-ful. By this criterion, one of
the first questions a pulpit committee might ask of a potential
pastor is, "What books have you read in the last couple of
days?" And on the basis of his answer an informed, thinking,
that is to say, educated, church, could practically decide
whether *he* could teach *them* anything.

Educating Christian man can be undertaken, of course,
without recourse to stories. It certainly has been, often enough,
in its short past. When it has used stories, it has linked them to
a study of the Christian faith, so that in the end the stories
serve merely to engage discussants in a lively rigged conversation that implacably proceeds to "But what has this got to
say to the Christian faith?" The final proposal offered in these
pages denies the effectiveness of this use of fiction and points
out the obscurantism that underlies it. The proposal proceeds
in the opposite direction. It suggests that as human beings
authors of fiction are quite as well loved as readers of fiction.
God has announced an indiscriminate love of the human race
in such uncompromising terms that we have got to allow for
the possibility that secular authors have dealings with God
even if they have never "darkened the door of the church."
The reading of fiction has the possibility of being a unique
charismatic event for the reader, in which he encounters his
future, if he stands ready to lay hold of it.

The uniqueness of this event comes out of the private inner
dwellings on himself that are the stuff of so much of the
lonely individual's life. Here a story grips him and holds him.
Here his own story—past, future, and now—bids his attention.
Here within his loneliness he knows that life is taken up with
decisions, risks, love-making, sacrifices, laughter, tears, effort,
enthusiasm, courage, and that it is mocked by indecision,
safety first, love-taking, insurance, fake belly laughs, Judas
tears, ease, drunkenness, and cowardice. Out of his loneliness
proceeds any risks he will ever take or any love that he will
ever make. And to the loneliness of the individual Christian
education can minister by informing it, through stories, of the

single overriding issue of the Christian faith: Will the lonely individual love his neighbor?

With the serious proposal that fiction be studied seriously in a thinking church, this book reaches its conclusion and its climax. The hard look that we have taken at the contemporary theory and performance of adult education in the church has not softened. The concession to sin and compromise with goals —presupposed by the proposal of contract groups and recouped somewhat by the inauguration of fiction study—do not thus diminish as concession or compromise. They have been made reluctantly but without apology. The proposals in which they are embodied will undoubtedly commend themselves to pastors and educators who have beforehand already assumed their proper educational function as thinkers. The proposals will as readily be dismissed by pastors and educators who consider thinking as a social reflex mechanism.

In the meantime, the lonely individual proceeds onward into his future. Will Christian education take proper account of him and his interminable thinking? Will Christian education aid, promote, and encourage his thinking, or will Christian education continue to evade him by use of its bag of dynamic tricks? This is the issue that this book has attempted to raise with both its analyses and proposals.

374
F94

111534